THE
EXECUTOR'S
HANDBOOK

The Daily Telegraph

THE EXECUTOR'S HANDBOOK

EVERYTHING YOU NEED TO KNOW ABOUT WILLS AND PROBATE

SECOND EDITION

Roger & Ann Taylor

The Institute of *In association with* Professional Willwriters

KOGAN PAGE

First published in 1997
Revised Edition 1998
Second Edition 1999

Kogan Page Limited
120 Pentonville Road
London N1 9JN

© The Institute of Professional Willwriters 1997, 1999

The right of Roger and Ann Taylor to be identified as authors of this work has been asserted by them in accordance with the Copyright, Designs and Patents Act 1988.

British Library Cataloguing in Publication Data

A CIP record for this book is available from the British Library.

ISBN 0 7494 3009 5

Typeset by Saxon Graphics Ltd, Derby
Printed and bound in Great Britain by Thanet Press Ltd, Margate

Contents

Contents

Making a Will
requires more than just beautiful handwriting

- It needs an understanding of the complexities very often necessary to ensure that this most important of legal documents will be capable of discouraging contentious action.
- It needs to be drafted in a way that will make its execution as simple as possible for your Executor.
- It needs to clearly state your wishes and requirements in order to provide your Executor with concise instructions.

If you agree that practicality is more important than beauty on this occasion, then you should consider asking a member of the IPW to visit you and assist in making your Will

IPW members are all required to:
- Pass stringent examinations before they are allowed into the Institute.
- Abide by the Code of Practice laid down for the protection of clients' rights.
- Give details of their fees and costs before visiting a client.
- Have Professional Indemnity Insurance approved by the IPW.

Why wait any longer –
telephone the IPW on 0800 074 5993 (Freephone)
Ask to be put in touch with an experienced Willwriter

INSTITUTE OF PROFESSIONAL WILLWRITERS

14 Foregate Street – Worcester – WR1 1DB

Telephone: 01905 611165

About the Authors

Roger Taylor
Educated at the Royal Masonic School, Roger's teachers greatly influenced an interest in research and writing. Many years in advertising and marketing, personnel selection and senior management in London and overseas followed. He has lectured internationally, designed and run training courses and was elected an FIPA. A few years ago he and Ann decided that Somerset was to be home, from where they pursue their writing and artistic careers.

Ann Taylor
Following a successful early career in business publishing in Fleet Street and then confidential government secretarial work, Ann obtained a B.Ed(Hons) at Reading University. She then taught Business Studies for 20 years at a senior level in both the state and independent sectors. More recently she has, theoretically though not actually, retired from teaching. Apart from concentrating on her writing, Ann is also an accomplished ceramic sculptor and her work sells worldwide.

Preface to Second Edition

There will always be Budget changes and new laws from time to time that affect the responsibilities of Executors and Administrators of Wills. This Second Edition of *The Executor's Handbook* reflects those up to and including the 1999 Budget.

Any Budget will clearly state changes to Inheritance Tax rates and perhaps other changes in the rules that will apply for the future. However, these are only briefly summarized on radio and television and in the following day's newspapers. There is usually, particularly these days, rather more in the 'small print'.

This new edition covers these issues as comprehensively as possible at the time of going to press and also reflects the positive responses that the authors have received to the original edition.

Roger and Ann Taylor

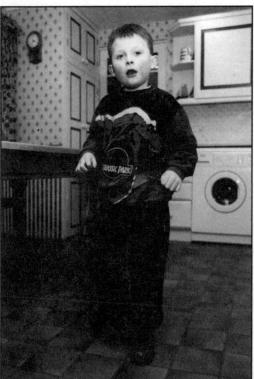

It took 4 years of hard work but Mark has learned to walk

At 6 weeks old Mark hated physical contact. He screamed when cuddled and arched his back.

At 18 months he could not creep, crawl and seemed 'switched off' from the world.

Nobody could say what was wrong or what to expect.

After 4 years of dedication Mark has been taught to walk. He is now a smiling, responsive child with a cheeky character.

BIBIC is a small but national charity which works in partnership with parents to improve hurt children's quality of life.

Don't just believe us:

'Nicholas would not be as he is today without the help of BIBIC' - Nicholas' Mum

'Rachel is calmer, happier and loving. She used to hate physical contact. I never thought she would put her arms around and give me a squeeze' - Mrs B

'Emily has come so far, her progress has been amazing'- Mrs Keats

'I cannot speak highly enough of BIBIC' - Mother of Charlotte, 3fi

**FREE information is available from: Caron Lane BSc, Head of Clinic
BIBIC - The British Institute for Brain Injured Children
Knowle Hall, Bridgwater, Somerset, TA7 8PJ**

**Tel: 01278 684 060 Fax: 01278 685 573 Email: info@BIBIC.org.uk
Registered charity no: 1057635
Founded in 1972**

Your legacy will help us help more children

Acknowledgements

Many people have helped us in the research and preparation of this book.

Our particular thanks go to Valerie Shiman, Errol Nott, John Ellershaw, Susan Ioannou and their colleagues in the Institute of Professional Willwriters. Also to Andrew Taylor, a practicing solicitor, for his most helpful and unstinting guidance on the many technicalities involved in such a project.

Thanks to the generosity of spirit of those who willingly shared their experiences, we have been privileged to enjoy a rich vein of personal reminiscences – from the sad to the downright funny – which have made the case histories so interesting. We hope that you will find them a valuable element of this book. Where you read words in quotation marks they are those spoken to us by our contributors. The only editing has been to tone down some of the language used on certain occasions!

These people were happy to share their experiences on the basis of their privacy being preserved. This we have respected, and always shall. It is usual to state at the start of a book that names used and situations described are fictitious. Here only the names are. We offer them our most sincere thanks.

HELP ONE OF THE UK'S FAVOURITE CHARITIES AND HAVE YOUR WILL MADE FOR FREE

Imperial Cancer Research Fund hopes Free Solicitors Service will boost legacy income

A man who left his local publican £15 to buy a bible *"so he can learn how Christ turned water into wine instead of the other way round"*, and the husband who left his assets to his wife on the condition she remarry *"so someone regrets my death"* are just two of the stranger things people have left in their Wills.

For those who want to take a more practical approach to Will making, the Imperial Cancer Research Fund's Free Solicitors Service is giving people the opportunity to leave money to a more worthwhile cause - helping fund the charity's vital £56 million a year cancer research programme.

The Imperial Cancer Research Fund, which carries out more than a third of all UK cancer research, has teamed up with local solicitors around the country to offer people the chance to make or update their Wills free of charge. Imperial Cancer hopes that through this service people will remember the charity in their Wills so that it can continue its work into the understanding, prevention, treatment and cure of cancer.

Patrick Latham, Head of the Legacy Administration at Imperial Cancer, explained why legacies are so important to the charity. He said: *"More than half our income is derived from what people leave us in their Wills. This money is a vital part of our income which is used by our scientists and doctors across the country who are involved in leading edge research."*

"Most of us know someone who has been affected by cancer and we hope that by offering people the chance to have their Wills made for free, they will thank us by leaving Imperial Cancer a gift in their Wills."

Patrick added: *"A legacy need not always be money. During my time with the Imperial Cancer Research Fund I have seen some amazing items bequeathed to us including:*

... a share of the royalties of Raphael Sabatini's books to the end of the century;

... Benjamin Britten and Wagner manuscripts;

... a brooch presented by Queen Victoria to Dame Clara Butt, a famous contralto from early this century;

... royalties from the music "Kiss Me Goodnight Sergeant Major."

Supporting the Imperial Cancer Research Fund's pioneering research programme by leaving a gift in your Will shows in a practical way that you care about those close to you and future generations. A leaflet explaining how you can get involved with the scheme is available from the Imperial Cancer Research Fund on **0171 269 3730**.

The Imperial Cancer Research Fund is dedicated to the understanding, prevention, treatment and cure of all forms of cancer. Its 1,000 scientists and doctors are at the forefront of the worldwide effort to defeat the disease. The charity relies overwhelmingly on voluntary funding to carry out its vital work.

For further information: Telephone: 0171 269 3730

Have you the will
to change their lives for the better?

Loneliness, despair, homelessness, hunger – maybe all they need is a little love.

Sadly, today so many people, both young and old are in such a desperate situation they need something a little more practical. Like a bed. Help with the shopping. A chat. Or just a welcoming cup of tea.

Every week, The Salvation Army cares for more than 60,000 people in the UK alone. We don't apportion blame, we don't moralise. We just roll our sleeves up and get on with it.

By leaving a legacy to The Salvation Army in your will you are doing more than helping us in our vital work, you are sowing a seed of kindness for people desperately in need.

To find out how you can leave a legacy to The Salvation Army, please write to us at:
The Salvation Army, FREEPOST KE3466, 101 Queen Victoria Street, London EC4B 4SR.

Thank you and God bless you.
The Salvation Army is a registered charity.

MAKE YOUR WILL, MAKE THEIR LIVES.   DTEH1

The Federation of British Artists

In 1961, a number of the leading art societies in the country joined to form the Federation of British Artists to promote the study and practice of fine art. In 1971, HM The Queen opened their galleries in the Mall, where they remain to this day. The nine societies forming the Federation are:

- **Royal Institute of Painters in Water Colours**
- **Royal Society of British Artists**
- **Royal Society of Marine Artists**
- **Royal Society of Portrait Painters**
- **Royal Institute of Oil Painters**
- **New English Art Club**
- **Pastel Society**
- **Society of Wildlife Artists**
- **Hesketh Hubbard Art Society**

It pursues its aims by providing facilities for, and encouragement to, practising artists, showing the work of the 650 member artists together with that of lesser known artists who have submitted work in the open sections, and encouraging learning and a wdier appreciaiton of the fine arts by the general public. This is done by staging exhibitors, drawing classes, demonstrations, workshops, and lectures in the   galleries.

Artists are encouraged by prizes, scholarships and awards. The galleries are let as reduced rates to colleges for their degree shows, and events such as the National Print Exhibition are staged by the Federation.

The Mall Galleries also provide a very large space for hire during the day and in the evenings. Situated at the end of the Mall by Trafalgar Square, they are perfectly located for easy access, giving hirers a prestigious and easily-recognised address in the very heart of London.

But despite, or perhaps because of, the Federation's insistence on teaching the traditional skills of drawing and painting, it receives no local, regional or Arts Council grant. All its income is derived from fees and rental charged, and enormous effort and ingenuity goes into maintaining the Mall's high standards. Lord Gowrie said that Arts organisations should either be very rich, or very poor and therefore funded; they should avoid just breaking even. The Federation justs breaks even, and has no resources to improve facilities or expand its activities, and indeed it is only by the remarkable dedication of its staff that it survives in the modern world.

From the public spectacle of the Royal Society of Portrait Painters opening day to the hushed concentration of a Hesketh Hubbard life drawing class, the Federation of British Artists at the Mall Galleries continues a provide a unique public service in the study and practice of fine art.

**17 Carlton House Terrace
London SW1Y 5BD
0171-930 6844**

LOOK & LEARN

THE FEDERATION OF BRITISH ARTISTS

We are an Educational Charity teaching the theory and
practice of painting, drawing sculpture and the decorative arts.
Where else can you look at work by Britains's leading traditional
artists and learn how to paint and draw, all in the same place?
At the Mall Galleries, the home of nine major
art societies.

The Federation receives no outside funding from any source.

We rely on the fees charged on the sale of works of art and the
letting of the gallery space.

Practical art teaching, concentrating on a solid basis in traditional
skills, is a fundamental part of good all-round education, both for
children and adults.
Please help us to continue with this work.

**Any bequest, however small, will be put to the best use to
encourage the largest number of people to benefit from our
programme of exhibitions and workshops.**

For further information please contact
John Molony or John Sayers at
Federation of British Artists 17 Carlton House Terrace
London SWIY 5BD
Tel **0171-930 6844**   Fax **0171-839 7830**
Charity No 200048

MALL GALLERIES   THE HOME OF BRITISH ART

A lasting gift
of hope...

Darren was born with Muscular
Dystrophy, and at the age of
seven life seemed a hopeless
ordeal as he struggled to cope in
a mainstream school full of
able-bodied pupils.

When at last he was referred to
a Shaftesbury school with spe-
cialist facilities and professional carers who understood his needs,
Darren began to thrive. He is now a happy, confident student, expecting
to gain good qualifications and fulfil his hopes of a successful career.

Darren's life was completely turned around by the care he received from
Shaftesbury - but to continue and develop our work we depend heavily
on the generosity of our supporters.

Please give a lasting gift of hope to other people like Darren by leaving a
legacy to Shaftesbury. See the feature opposite to find out more about
our work, or please telephone our Legacy Officer on 0181 239 5569.

(Photograph posed by model and name changed to protect confidentiality)

...your legacy can
help transform lives

Shaftesbury

150 years of Christian care in action

Registered Charity No 221948
Registered in England No 38751

xx

The Shaftesbury Society -
over 150 years of Christian care in action

The Shaftesbury Society is one of the country's leading Christian caring charities - supporting people with a disability and those on low incomes, helping them find security, self-worth and significance.

Shaftesbury began life over 150 years ago as The Ragged School Union, founded in 1844 under the influence of the Victorian social reformer the 7th Earl of Shaftesbury. He successfully campaigned for changes to many laws that still affect our lives, including those preventing women and children working long hours in factories and mines. The first Ragged Schools were run for the children of families who were too poor to afford proper clothes, let alone an education.

Today, children and young people with a disability go to one of Shaftesbury's schools and colleges, which provide the specialist education to equip them for maximum independence both now and in the future. Shaftesbury manages a wide range of accommodation within the community, enabling adults with a disability to live in a homely environment. We also support people with a disability in their own home.

Shaftesbury employs church-based Community Workers, who encourage and enable others to make a difference in their local community. Some churches also work in partnership with Shaftesbury to run community centres, nurseries and day care centres.

For people living on the lowest incomes, Shaftesbury's Resources Centre brings quality used furniture within reach to make unfurnished accommodation into a real home, and our Latymer Training project gives those facing long-term unemployment the skills and confidence to get into employment or voluntary work. Shaftesbury's Homeless Service provides shelter and professional support, helping young people who have experienced homelessness to find stable accommodation and employment.

We rely heavily on donations and legacies to finance our work. For more information about ways of supporting Shaftesbury or any aspect of our work, please contact us at the address below.

The Shaftesbury Society
16 Kingston Road, London SW19 1JZ
Tel 0181 239 5555
Fax 0181 239 5580

Registered Charity No 221948   Registered in England No 38751

USPG - Where balance sheets add up to something different....

"When I qualified," laughs accountant Michael Hart, "I'd never have believed it if you had told me that I would find a job that brought together my accounting qualification, my Christian faith and my interest in music."

Michael is USPG's chief accountant. Before he came to USPG, he worked for a major department store.

"It was great working in the West End," says Michael. "There was a real buzz in the atmosphere, but somehow I still felt that something was missing."

"I think the issue was that I wanted figures to mean more than just profits and losses on a balance sheet. I wanted them to make a real difference to people's lives," reflects Michael.

"Now, I know that when a sum is left as a legacy or given as a donation to USPG, it does just that."

As sharp as any accountant when discussing figures, Michael comments, "If you ask me what's the first thing that comes to my mind when I hear any figure – maybe '£30,000' – I'd say how funding from USPG helps the local Church run vital projects in Bangladesh. And it's not just one type of work: education, Mission programmes, women's vocational training, health classes – they're all helped by our grants.

"Another figure? Say '£165,000'.... I'd think of the fifty people from different parts of the world who live and study together at the United College of the Ascension, the exciting international college we share with the Methodist Church in Birmingham. That really is Christian mission in action.

"And if you up the figure to '£230,000', I'd think of clinics and hospitals. You only have to read the letters and reports that come to us from some of the poorest parts of Africa to know that USPG support makes all the difference in life-and-death situations."

Michael pauses. "Of course, that's just part of the story. I know at the end of the day that without the people who remember USPG in their wills and send us donations, we couldn't work for the worldwide Church as we do. I only hope that people will carry on supporting us so that we can keep on going into the next century, which incidentally will be our fourth!"

A legacy of pride

We have good reason to be proud of those who have defended our freedom both at home and around the world. And it's not just those men and women in uniform to whom we owe such gratitude, but to their families as well.

Many find themselves fighting battles on many different fronts. Serving and ex-Service personnel and their families frequently face special difficulties and SSAFA Forces Help has been there for more than 100 years to defend them against illness, poverty and need. We offer lifelong friendship, practical help and emotional support to every serving and ex-Service man and woman and their dependants, in need.

To continue this support, we depend almost entirely on your generosity. This is where a legacy* really can make a difference.

To help you prepare a will we have produced a useful brochure, available free from:
The Legacy Officer, SSAFA Forces Help, 19 Queen Elizabeth Street, London SE1 2LP or by speaking to us on 0171 403

Yes, I would like to consider making a bequest to SSAFA Forces Help. Please send me further information about the Association and your "Legacy Fact File" (including A Guide to Making your Will).

Name ....

Address ....

....

....**☰FORCES**

SSAFA Forces Help,   **SSAFA Help**
19 Queen Elizabeth Street
LONDON SE1 2LP
Telephone: 0171 403 8783   (26)

* You may wish also to send a donation.
If so, please make your cheque payable to
SSAFA Forces Help
and send to the above address. Thank you.

The Soldiers, Sailors, Airmen and
Families Association - Forces Help
Registered Charity Number 210760. Est 1885

Introduction

Reading this you probably fall into one of two categories.

EITHER

You have been asked by someone you know well to be one of the Executors of his or her Will. It will usually be by someone quite close to you, a relative or good friend. Perhaps secretly reluctant, you accept. You may privately feel very flattered, or you may simply find it difficult to refuse without causing real, or imagined, offence.

Whatever the initial reaction, you have agreed and are then named, alongside one or more other Executors. It does not matter at this stage whether or not you might be a beneficiary. You are quite entitled to be, though unless specifically authorized in the Will, you may not make charges against the estate for your services, but you may be reimbursed for proper expenses.

Unless the person who has asked you knows that they are terminally ill, you see the whole issue as one of 'sensible provision' being made for an event that will not be happening until a long time in the future. The mechanics of it all probably don't bother you much at this stage. On the other hand you might simply be browsing and have picked this volume off the shelf in order to acquaint yourself with the nature of the responsibilities that you might have at some time. Just idle curiosity.

OR

You may just have found that you have an immediate job to do as an Executor and are in urgent need of advice and guidance, quite possibly in circumstances that are both distressing and stressful.

Whichever is the case, you have, or will have, an important task. It need not be daunting and this reference book sets out to guide you through the processes in as simple a way as possible, avoiding legal jargon, or at least making it understandable.

In most of the instances where you are likely to be involved you should find matters fairly straightforward. Where there might be a need for professional legal advice you can be guided by this book to help you avoid unnecessary expense.

Reading on, inevitably you are going to find repetitious use of words such as emotion and stress. We make no apology for this; there are few words that are available in our language to describe what happens when explaining how people react before and after death. No excuses are made for the repetitions.

In the course of writing this book many people have helped us by giving of their time to discuss their personal experiences. The case histories have been fully researched and are based on events as they were experienced. They are anonymous but real. The words used are those spoken in our interviews.

The names used have been 'invented' by the authors to preserve the privacy of our 'contributors'. Inevitably, someone reading this guide might see their own name in print! Rest assured that that is quite coincidental. We are not given the opportunity to choose our names at birth. Most of us live with them throughout our lives. We do not have doubles in personalities, or circumstances, just in names!

Near tragedies have occurred as a result of no Will being found. Even where there is a Will, great anxiety can be caused by it being badly written, ambiguous, spiteful or even malicious. Family feuds, subterfuge and intrigue might make a good plot for a novelist or playwright but can be hell for those that are left living with them.

One distressingly consistent element was hearing of the anguish caused by the deceased leaving personal or business affairs in a mess. In small family-owned and family-run ventures this often seems to happen; hidden debts, poor record-keeping, carelessness, to name a few.

It can be seen that the single most obvious thread running through the majority of the case histories is the matter of family 'discussion' of one sort or another. After the death of someone close, whether popular or not, the bereaved are usually saddened or shocked. (Isn't it amazing how even enemies are often described as 'not being too bad, really' after their death?) Whatever the emotions, the last thing that people need is to have to cope with the slings and arrows of outrageous relatives and claimants.

The varied, real-life case histories are linked to relevant chapters throughout the book and it is hoped that you will be able to relate to one or more of these.

As society has evolved, and continues to evolve, our attitudes towards such matters as divorce and illegitimacy, for example, once spoken of only behind closed doors, have gradually changed. Cohabiting couples, once regarded as 'living in sin' and shunned by society, are now often accepted; indeed, the word 'partner' seems almost to be in more common usage than the words 'husband' and 'wife'. Our laws have been amended, over the years, to reflect and support such social changes and they too are subject to change following, for instance, successful and hugely expensive test cases. Sadly, we live in times where expensive litigation, beyond the means of most of us, is too often seen as the first resort rather than the last.

As Executor, you will no doubt find yourself relying on your own value judgements when dealing with potentially awkward situations; it is hoped that reading the examples given in the case histories will be helpful to you in this task.

In each case history we have quoted parts of actual conversations that took place, preserving only the identities of the people concerned. The problems that they faced illustrate the dilemmas encountered, and some of the emotional aspects involved.

In every meeting we have had with those who generously were prepared to share their experiences, the emotion and stress were evident or barely suppressed. At least, in most of them the conclusion has been businesslike and satisfactory. New lives have been built out of the sadness of having lost a dear one.

We hope that the guidance and advice that this book offers will help the process go smoothly, and as quickly as possible, for you and all those you represent.

Your legacy could give little Harry a brighter, happier future

Harry is just one of thousands of children around the world suffering through poverty, war and exploitation.

Thanks to the generous people who leave legacies to Save the Children, our child projects give them the chance of a brighter future.

From emergency relief in places like Honduras and Sudan, to projects in the UK helping young people tackle the many problems they face, we are making a real difference. With your support today, we can do even more.

Please leave a legacy to Save the Children in your Will and give children like Harry a brighter future.

For your free Legacy Information Pack, send your name and address details to: Paula Chabrel, Legacy Manager, Save the Children, 8950057, FREEPOST, London SE5 8BR.

Or you can order your Pack from our website: http://www.scfuk.org.uk

Alternatively call our Legacy Helpline **0171 703 8799**

Save the Children
Registered Charity No. 213890

Save the Children

Throughout the world, innocent children and their families face a daily struggle to survive poverty, oppression and disaster. Without help, their future looks bleak.

Save the Children is the UK's leading international children's charity, working to create a better future for children, both in the UK and around the world.

Legacies make up one third of Save the Children's total voluntary income; they are a vital part of its funds. That's why Save the Children relies on supporters who choose to give in this special way.

The money Save the Children receives through legacies goes directly to help children - wherever the need is greatest. This could be an emergency, providing medical care for children in Honduras, or it could be a long-term project, such as addressing the problems of child labour in Pakistan.

In Save the Children's hands, your legacy will become a permanent gift of hope to generations of children, their families and communities around the world.

If you haven't yet made a Will, it is easy to arrange. Send for Save the Children's free Legacy Information Pack containing the booklet 'A Guide to Making or Changing your Will' - an easy to follow guide on protecting the people and causes you care for.

If you would like any advice on making or changing your Will, Save the Children can arrange for one of its Legacy Advisers to meet you. He/She will visit you at a time and place that's convenient to you, and can help you with all aspects of making a Will.

Your local Legacy Adviser can also explain in more detail how your legacy will help children across the world, and show you videos and literature about the work of Save the Children. He/She can even put you in touch with local solicitors who support Save the Children.

**For further information
Please contact
Save the Children**

**Telephone: 0171 703 5400
Facsimile: 0171 703 2278**

WWF is the world's leading conservation organisation. It is dedicated to the protection of the planet's endangered species and their habitats...

Founded in 1961, WWF has become the world leader through the establishment of national parks and habitat restoration programmes; working closely with governments and local communities, internationally, to improve conservation policies; thwarting illegal wildlife trade and working to enforce environmental laws; building relationships with other conservation organisations and, finally, through education and awareness.

Since 1961, WWF has funded 12,600 projects in 154 countries throughout the world. In addition, WWF-UK has funded more than 2,500 conservation projects in the UK alone, saving hundreds of important sites including woodlands, meadows, cliffs, marshes, rivers and estuaries.

The charity's mission is to stop, and eventually reverse, the accelerating degradation of the planet's natural environment, and to help build a future in which humans live in harmony with nature.

You can share in that mission by remembering WWF in your Will.

A NEW AND SIMPLE WAY TO MAKE A LASTING GIFT TO CHARITY...

Many people want to leave a gift to charity in their Will but worry about how much they can afford.

Leaving a *percentage* of your estate, rather than a fixed amount, means that no matter what happens in the years ahead, the amount bequeathed will *always* be appropriate to your financial situation at the time.

Send for our FREE guide to making and updating a Will. It tells you when - and how - to change your Will and also outlines how you can leave the most lasting gift of all by making a bequest to WWF-UK.

You can request your copy by phoning Sally Burrowes, Head of Legacies on

01483 426445

or write to her at WWF-UK, FREEPOST, Panda House, Godalming, Surrey GU7 1BR quoting reference EH1.

Registered Charity Number: 201707

EH1

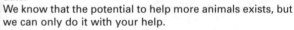

1

About Wills and Probate

What is a Will?

The most straightforward definition of a Will is from the dictionary: 'directions, usually written, in legal form for disposition to be made of a person's property after their death'.

Most of us can readily conjure images of Dickensian scenes often portrayed in plays and films where, amid high drama, the family is summoned to a solicitor's office to hear the reading of 'The last Will and Testament of the dear departed . . .' This is always done in solemn and serious manner and, in the drama, is usually the precursor of bitter family feuds, murder plots and more. Translate the setting to modern dress and the drama might be remarkably similar.

However, in real life today it is seldom like that – hopefully, at least, not to the extent of plotting murder. Or can it be? Even that is not unknown. Unfortunately, though, much bitterness is sometimes caused by perceived injustices in the content of a Will when published.

A Will is the only document that speaks from the grave. It is also the way of trying to ensure that what you want to happen after your death does so. It is also a way of ensuring that should you die young, the guardians of your offspring are those of your choice rather than those that might be selected by an impersonal state organization. Not least, it can reduce, or even avoid, inheritance tax.

Why is it made?

Sensibly, everyone should make a Will, though not enough do and the 'legacy' they leave can sometimes be very painful for

9

those left behind, who end up clearing up a very messy situation which could have been avoided. Case History 1, given at the end of this chapter, demonstrates just such a situation.

Too often people underestimate the value of their possessions, and simply fail to consider the effect of their death on others who might in some way be dependent upon them. People marrying young and starting out with little or nothing cannot see the purpose of having a Will. Anyway, at a young age it seems a very morbid thing to do. They imagine that that is something that you do when you are older. And then probably forget!

The cost might seem offputting anyway. Solicitors' fees for such work are often high. Of course, for the serious-minded, even at a young age, preprepared forms can be bought from stationers, properly filled in, *and properly witnessed*! These would be quite valid. However, a professional advisor will always help you produce a better Will and there will be less chance of any misinterpretation. Increasingly today, people use one of the small number of specialist professional organizations offering the services of qualified, independent Willwriters. Their fixed-scale costs will usually be substantially less than those of solicitors, and often they will offer a very personal home service. Their independence means that they have no long-term interest in fees that solicitors can charge by offering to act as an Executor. There is more objectivity.

These independents will be available to help their clients at intervals through their careers and changing personal circumstances as, hopefully, assets are accumulated. They can advise on the effects of changing tax laws and other events, impartially. Their role is to advise and guide the Testator so that the job of the Executors, when the time comes, is as uncomplicated as possible.

For this reason the Institute of Professional Willwriters is a co-sponsor of this book.

Just what have I let myself in for?

While agreeing to be an Executor, you naturally would not seek to be embroiled in a confusing, even messy, process of administration. On assuming this role you probably quite rightly expect that no major complications can be foreseen. As years pass, however, many events could change the situation and if you are familiar with such events within the family of the deceased you may well have reason to suspect problems ahead.

There is no legal requirement to inform Executors of any of the conditions of a Will at the time of it being written and witnessed, though often the broad outlines of its content and intent might or might not have been communicated.

There must be at least two witnesses to any Will, although the Testator may appoint more witnesses if desired. *Neither of the witnesses can be beneficiaries, spouses of beneficiaries or an Executor or spouse of an Executor*; and in cases where such witnesses have been used, whilst the Will remains valid at death, any legacy is automatically forfeited and the Executor, whilst being able to carry out his duties, would only be able to claim reasonable costs. If the Executor is a professional person who might reasonably expect to charge fees, then any clause in the Will allowing for such professional management fees to be charged against the Estate is no longer valid.

Is is essential that both Testator and witnesses should sign the Will in each other's presence. Witnesses to a Will have no right to read the contents before they sign. All they are being required to witness is the Testator actually signing the Will, not the content unless the Testator wishes otherwise.

Understanding how a Will might be written

As stated above, there are few legal requirements regarding the validity of a Will.

The writing of one does not have to be done by a solicitor. Simple, clear use of language that can be understood will clearly communicate intentions. It seldom needs to be phrased in traditional legal jargon, much of which was developed in centuries much earlier than ours. In the latter part of the 1990s there are positive campaigns for the long overdue use of plain English in legal documents of all kinds, from hire purchase agreements to Wills. We must hope the campaigners succeed. Paragraphs and pages of unnecessary small print and tortuous language have no place in our world. It seems that their only

Friends of the Elderly

Friends of the Elderly meets the needs of frail and disadvantaged elderly people, supporting them both in their homes and in the Friend's own residential homes.

Friends of the Elderly, founded in 1905, is widely respected for its exceptional residential and nursing homes and invaluable welfare work, supporting elderly people on very low income who are struggling physically or financially to remain independent in their own homes. The Friends disperses grants for mobility aids, household repairs and help with heating for those on low incomes and are developing home help, befriending and personal care services in the community.

For those who become too frail to manage alone, the Friends provide residential homes based on Christian values with nursing care on site. Upgrading all homes to meet the needs of the increasingly frail, together with the provision of safe and homely dementia care, are central objectives of the Friend's strategy to meet the needs of the elderly today.

Friends of the Elderly is uniquely in a position to provide a continuum of care responding to the clearly expressed wishes of the elderly to stay in their own homes. This ranges from cash grants, preventative home care services and practical home help, respite, residential nursing and dementia care in the Friend's own Homes. Sheltered accommodation into which care can be delivered by the Friends, if and when needed, is also in the pipeline.

Preventative services enable older people to retain their independence and prevent an escalation of future care needs, dependence and costs. This is especially needed to support carers of people with dementia who live at home and for people in the early stages of dementia who are living alone.

FRIENDS OF THE ELDERLY

Caring for elderly people in their homes and our own.

Charity Number: 226064

Please be a Friend
to the Elderly

Friends of the Elderly founded in 1905 to befriend and support destitute families

The needs of the elderly are changing. Older people want to remain independent in their own homes so Friends of the Elderly is meeting those needs through befriending and home care services, with grants to those on low incomes to help cope with problems ranging from long-term mobility and home repairs to immediate, basic daily needs.

The Friends provide residential homes, based on Christian values, with nursing care on site and is in process of upgrading all homes to meet the needs of the increasingly frail, together with the provision of safe and homely dementia care.

Please remember **Friends of the Elderly** in your will.

FRIENDS
OF THE ELDERLY

To discuss how your legacy can help, telephone in confidence:
Caroline Atkinson, Friends of the Elderly
40-42 Ebury Street, London SW1W 0LZ
Telephone: 0171 730 8263 Fax: 0171 259 0154

purpose is to confuse us by preserving legal myths. Society must have laws, and therefore lawyers, for its own good, but they should be readily comprehensible.

Organizations like the Institute of Professional Willwriters with qualified members provide advice and service just as well as a solicitor and will probably charge less. An advantage of using independents is that they put no pressure on the Testator to appoint them as an Executor. Solicitors have been known to do this, hiding behind the myth that only they are really qualified to handle the administration, trusts and whatever other affairs the deceased might leave on his or her death. Handling administration and probate is an important source of income for legal firms, large and small, and their charges are usually high.

It is important to be aware that every Estate has some value, however grand or modest. Where Trusts are to be set up then it is important to take professional advice.

A solicitor drafting a Will where that solicitor, or the firm, is named as an Executor properly should, in a separate letter by way of a written agreement with the Testator, state the scale fees they will charge for their professional role. You can expect to find a phrase such as, 'fees at the rate which applies at the time when such services are required'. Obviously a Will written with the help of a solicitor, naming that solicitor or legal firm as an Executor, might well have been done many years ago and their hourly rates will have risen, probably dramatically, with the passage of time.

Banks have trustee departments that will offer their services as Executors, though usually only for fairly substantial Estates, and they are generally the most expensive. They should provide a scale of their fees which should be written into any such contract.

Well chronicled are examples of beneficiaries receiving little or nothing after the professional, acting as an Executor, has taken fees. This is not to say that all are unscrupulous, but two of the case histories here show graphically how professionals have protracted the administration process. Of course this means the fee 'meter' continues to clock up. More importantly it usually means that the grief and distress already being suffered by the loss of a loved one are unnecessarily prolonged. Every letter or phone call referring to the deceased is almost bound to take its toll and the longer it goes on the worse it gets.

It is a fact that in 1996 the Law Society commissioned a leading market research company to establish the attitudes of a sample of the clients of their members to the quality of service that Law Society members had offered them. They seemed *pleased* with the findings 'that *only 25 per cent* of people were *dissatisfied*' – their quote on a BBC programme. To most of us this would be an unpalatably high figure and an admission of serious failings. One of the most frequently quoted complaints was of their role as Executors – the unnecessary, distressing delays and high costs!

At the end of the book you will find a glossary of terms to help you understand some of the terms and phrases you might come up against if you are having to deal with the legal profession. It should help you save both time and money.

In Chapter 3 the Executors' responsibilities in such matters will be discussed further. It is not a matter to dwell on now, however. As presenters say at the end of the crime programmes that pervade our TV screens these days: 'Don't have sleepless nights...' You should find it a satisfying task which, even if it is a bit pernickety at times, you will ultimately be pleased to have undertaken and proud to have performed successfully. In most cases you will be helping close family or friends. They will to a large extent be depending on you for support and advice; you will take some of their burden from them. Doubtless that was why you were asked in the first place – someone reliable, sensible and able to deal with the rather tedious duties that become the role of most Executors. However, you are entitled to refuse to act, as explained at the end of Chapter 2.

You could, of course, find yourself in a situation where it is not a direct family matter. It could be that, after the death of a friend with whom contact had lessened over the passage of time, you find you had long ago been nominated as an Executor in a Will written maybe even two decades ago and never altered. It is even possible that you were never consulted in the first place.

Another possibility is that while you may have been aware of the terms of a Will to which you agreed to be an Executor some years ago, this has subsequently been rewritten several times without you being informed. Although Codicils to an original Will can be added at any time and are valid if properly witnessed, we strongly advise against this. The best practice is to completely rewrite the Will, even if only a small section is being changed, and it is unwise to do this without proper guidance. With the ready availability of today's personal computers and word-processors the simple change of a paragraph or two in a Will is a simple, quick, inexpensive process. The signing of the new version must, of course, be, witnessed in the usual way as described earlier in this chapter.

In Case History 2, at the end of this chapter, the Codicil left by the deceased can be seen to have caused even more family dissension in an already fraught situation.

What is Probate?

As explained, an Executor's duties and responsibilities start at the moment of the person's death. Even though the Will has yet to be proved as required legally, the Executor's authority to act is absolute. When the Will is finally proved, the Executor is issued with a Grant of Probate which confirms the power to act that he has already been exercising. Only a solicitor, barrister or Notary Public can charge the Estate for obtaining probate.

Alternatively, in the event of no Will being found, a Grant of Letters of Administration may have to be applied for. They could also be necessary if the named Executors cannot, or will not, act, perhaps having predeceased or formally renounced the arrangement. Here it will probably be a near relative who will apply for the Letters to allow them to handle the administration of the deceased's affairs as specified in the Will. You can read more about this in Chapter 2.

Where do I find the Will?

When you are nominated, always assuming that you remember being asked, then do try to establish where you will be able to find the Will when the need arises. As the years go by you might casually, without being morbid, enquire as to its whereabouts and make sure you will be able to gain access when required. As a document it has no validity until the death of the person making the Will – the Testator. It then becomes extremely important and the Testator should have informed the Executors at the time of making the Will as to where it can be found when needed. It is good practice for the Will draughtsman to write to the Executors, confirming where the Will is to be kept and advising how it can be obtained when the Testator dies.

There are many bizarre stories of the search for a Will. If you do not know in advance where to look, you might have to trawl many different sources.

If the Will is kept locked up at home or in an office, then you should have been made aware of how to gain access quickly to the key or safe combination code.

If it has been lodged with a solicitor, bank, The Record Keeper's Department, Principal Registry of the Family Division (First Avenue House, 42–49 High Holborn, London WC1V 6NP), or other place of safekeeping, then the Testator should have been given a certificate of registry or other piece of paper acknowledging the deposit. You will need this, together with proof of your identity and often a copy of the death certificate to obtain release.

Just because such an organization has been storing the document, though not an Executor, does not mean that you are in any way obliged to use the services that they will undoubtedly offer and try persuasively to press on you. They might have a right to charge for past storage services and this would be a charge against the Estate. Do make quite sure though that this service was not paid for in advance at the time the Will was written. If it was then a receipt should have been issued. It is quite common practice for advance payment to be made and the Estate could be in danger of being charged twice. Establish the situation immediately and negotiate a fee if appropriate. You don't want a surprise bill coming in at a later stage, possibly after the Estate has been wound up.

It is not impossible that the nominated Executor so entrusted has died or moved away. Such matters are not necessarily left well organized. In recent years many solicitors' firms have been sold; premises and documents moved. The new keepers may be unable to trace the Will you need. This should never happen, of

FUNERAL PLANNING

We all know that making funeral arrangements is not top of most people's list of things to do. But by approaching it in the right way, it doesn't have to be a morbid task and will actually save friends and family a lot of distress when you're gone.

By planning for your funeral now, you can be sure of three important benefits. Firstly, the peace of mind that the arrangements are taken care of financially which, depending on the chosen plan, is a sensible investment. The certainty that your wishes will be carried out at your funeral. And finally, perhaps most importantly, the distress and worry of this task has been taken away from those close to you.

If you do decide to take care of your own funeral expenses, there are now several options available; funeral bonds, pre-payment plans, insurance policies and high interest savings accounts. It is important that you consider each one and think about which of the benefits is most important to you before deciding on the plan for you.

For many people, funeral bonds are the best option as not only are they unaffected by inflation, they also allow you to plan all the details of your funeral in advance, not just the payment. Most funeral bonds guarantee these main benefits and the Co-operative Funeral Bond, from Co-operative Funeral Service for example, is becoming increasingly popular. However, the details of every bond varies and it is vital that, as with any financial investment, you are sure of a number of key points before making a commitment.

- When examining different schemes, check that all elements of a funeral cost will be covered by the bond. Funeral costs are split into two parts; fees for professional services rendered directly by the funeral director and fees paid on your behalf by the funeral director, ie disbursements. Many bonds set a limit on the amount payable against disbursements which could lead to a shortfall in the payment at the time of death. The Co-operative Funeral Bond will, however, cover the full cost of the disbursements which were specified at the time of purchase.

- Ensure the bond monies are held in a separate and reputable trust, such as The Royal Bank of Scotland Plc who are Custodian Trustee for the Co-operative Funeral Bonds. Equally important is to check that the plan provider belongs to one of the relevant professional associations. The Co-operative Funeral Bond, for example, comes with the support of Funeral Planning Council.

- Finally, always ask that if you change your mind, you can withdraw your money with full refund or nominal administration fee.

Being aware of the advantages of paying for a funeral now, choosing the right plan for you, and thinking of this as an extension of your existing personal finance plans can only be to the benefit of you and your family.

Are you prepared for life after death?

Preparing for life after death.

Most people leave their family to bear the burden of making decisions at a very distressing time. Statistics show that 95% of people who pass away, leave their loved ones to make the necessary arrangements.

Unnecessarily.

Because a Co-operative Funeral Bond allows you to sort out any problems when it's not too late to tell your family what you want.

Not only will you receive a maximum of understanding, integrity and trust, with a minimum of fuss. But you pay today's price for something that won't happen for many more years to come. To make it even easier, you can pay by instalments.

Think about it.

Life's a lot less worrying when you know what's going to happen after you're gone.

For more information Telephone
0800 25 55 25

co-operative
Funeral service

☑ **Yes! Please send me more information on The Co-operative Funeral Bond.**

Surname_____

First Name_____

Address_____

_____

_____ Postcode_____

Telephone_____ Date of Birth ____ / ____ / ____

Once you have completed this form please send to: The Co-operative Funeral Bond, FREEPOST NWW 11102, Rochdale, Lancs OL11 1YF.

EH 1

course. However, it might just happen to you! We all know Sod's Law.

A prime example is a story that we, the co-authors, tell against ourselves. It serves as a graphic example. At one stage when researching one of the case histories it occurred to us that we ought to look at our own Wills, just out of interest. We found a handwritten note on the face of an envelope containing our birth certificates, marriage certificate and some other important documents. Written on the envelope was, 'Wills with XYZ solicitors', and the town where they were based. They had handled the sale of our previous house and the purchase of our present home.

XYZ firm of solicitors took ages to reply to the request for the release of our Wills. When they did respond, saying that they could find no records, we were inclined to blame them – they had moved their offices in the meantime. Would they have been quicker if there had been a death? After lengthy telephone conversations we began to wonder if we could have made an error. It transpired that we had. Another phone call established that our Wills were held by the solicitors, many miles away, who had acted for us on the purchase of the previous home some years before – huge personal embarrassment!

If we had made a mistake over where our Wills were held, we certainly had no documents acknowledging their deposit. Further enquiries indicated that they had never been issued – a salutary lesson. Some people leave their Will in a safety deposit box at their bank. This has caused problems on their death, as a bank will not release the contents of the box until Probate has been granted! Obviously, without the original Will, Probate cannot be applied for or obtained!

The incident does, though, demonstrate the onus on an Executor to find a Will. In this instance a scribbled note looked authoritative. We are alive and able to retrace our actions over the last however many years. An Executor, without the detailed knowledge of the deceased's past dealings, might have to dig deep into the past to find the Will. If it is not immediately traceable then you must look to when the Testator last moved home or when there was some other major change in lifestyle such as marriage or remarriage. Such an event is often a prime clue, as many people tend to think about Wills, and are encouraged to do so by their solicitors when handling the sale and purchase of a property. They might, as we did, move again a very few years later. We remembered that we had rewritten our Wills quite recently prior to this move though we could not remember exactly when. We saw no compelling reason to do so again. Why spend more with a solicitor than the inevitable costs associated with moving home anyway?

Remember that it is your duty to take possession of the Will immediately on proof of your right to it and then act according to its terms as you think most appropriate. You may well be confident that you can handle matters without incurring expensive professional fees. If at a later stage you decide that there is a requirement for such help then you can make that choice at the time.

If you choose to do so then you should be quite clear in your mind exactly what professional legal help you will require. You will quite probably already have done much of the groundwork and are just seeking technical advice on some issue that you do not understand or feel unable to deal with. In these circumstances your local Citizens' Advice Bureau could assist without charge. Most solicitors will want to take over the whole process. This can be very costly and it is quite likely that you are able to provide the required information which otherwise would take many expensive hours of their time to research. You will have done quite a lot of their work for them. Asking for a quote for a particular aspect or aspects of their service will help to pin the solicitor to a fixed price. This is important as there are many stories to be heard where lawyers' costs have got out of hand. If you feel that the solicitors' attitude to the costs that might be incurred is very vague at the first meeting and this concerns you, then remember that there are many others to chose from and perhaps you should consult with others before committing. You'll probably find it will be less expensive to go ... *à la carte* rather than *table d'hôte*.

How do I know it is the 'Last' Will?

Once you do have the Will to hand it is very important that you do everything in your power to establish that it genuinely is the 'last' or only Will made by the deceased.

In looking for reassurance about a Will being the definitive one, try to take a few moments to consider the life and career of the deceased. People who take the care to write a Will are often those who will rewrite, perhaps several times as their financial, marital or emotional circumstances change – often as a combination of all three. Family feuds do not only happen in fiction. The emotional scene often portrayed on film, 'I'll cut *them* out of my Will', does happen in reality. The emotion is often short-lived, though aggrieved and determined folk may well carry out such threats.

The Last Will can be a minefield. In extreme circumstances you might be faced with one that is contested and this is covered in our case histories. If, on first reading, you suspect that it might be an old one, since superseded, then you should search further. A more recent one might have been written and lodged in a different place, the former having been forgotten.

Why the rush to find the Will?

One very important reason for you knowing the Will's whereabouts very soon after death is to establish the deceased's wishes regarding disposal of the body. Often, for example, instructions will be included for funeral arrangements, specific burial wishes or what should be done with the ashes after cremation. Perhaps there has been a stated desire for the body, or parts of it, to be gifted for medical purposes. Medical authorities have rarely been consulted in advance in these cases but in the event of death, particularly if unexpected and away from a hospital environment, then action needs to be taken very quickly. More aspects of this subject in your role as an Executor will be discussed in Chapter 2, though it is worth noting here that after death the body no longer belongs to the Testator.

Lost Wills

If you understand that a Will had been written and you find that it has been lost or accidentally destroyed it is possible to obtain probate of a copy or reconstruction provided an order is first obtained. The procedure is set out in the Non-Contentious Probate Rules 1987, rule 54. The same procedure is used where probate of an oral Will is sought.

This can become quite complex and technical and it is recommended that if you find yourself in this situation you should consult a solicitor.

Although this might sound technical and complex, if you decide to instruct a solicitor the application will be prepared and an Order applied for on your behalf. If you are making a personal application, the Probate Registry staff will draft all the papers and apply for the Order for you.

What if I am expected to be Executor *and* Trustee *and/or* Guardian?

In some 90 per cent of Wills written by younger parents one or more Executor is also nominated as a Trustee and/or Guardian for their offspring to cover the possibility of the sudden death of both parents. This will usually be for a fixed period until their sons, daughters or other people specified achieve a certain age. In some cases, however – and this is so particularly in the event of a beneficiary being mentally handicapped or otherwise disabled – the Trustee will have a responsibility for the management of some of that person's financial affairs for their lifetime.

Will I be able to cope with all this?

To be of real help in such circumstances can be most satisfying personally. By reducing stress in others you will know that you can be of great help in a way that is often hard to quantify. You probably never thought of it this way but you will be fulfilling the wishes of the deceased – as they intended.

Chapter 2 advises you on the initial course of events. For necessary reasons this is usually the most intensely time-consuming period though everyone will want it over as soon as possible. Perhaps you might not be involved in all aspects between the death and the funeral, for a variety of very practical reasons. You may be asked by the immediate family to leave these matters to them. However, as an Executor you should be available to make sure that the wishes and directions of the deceased are respected and help the bereaved as soon as possible if you can, though in this you have a right to exercise discretion, as will be explained.

Also in Chapter 2 we explain what you need to do if you no longer wish to be involved. In all probability, however, and with the help and encouragement of this book, you will feel that you have some 'duty' to help the Testator's survivors, or perhaps an interest as a beneficiary will help you decide that you will proceed with the responsibility.

The powers and duties that go with your role once the funeral is over will be covered in detail in Chapter 3 and subsequently. What you do and where you might be able to help emotionally over the first few hours and days is going to be crucial, of course, but it is equally essential to try to start on a businesslike footing as finances are often very much an issue in the early days. This is yet another of the many reasons why it is so important to have the Will to hand at the earliest possible stage.

However, the main duties of the Executor are in the longer term, but not one hopes for *too* long! They are the straight-forward management of the deceased's Estate through to Probate – usually largely an administrative and bookkeeping exercise that most will not find too complicated. This book is to guide you through those processes to help ensure that they are neither too onerous nor more protracted than need be.

What is an 'Estate'?

Don't be misled or daunted by the frequent use of the word 'Estate'. It is simply used to describe the sum total of what a person owns and is not just associated with castles, mansions and acres of rolling countryside. A useful checklist is provided on pages 78–79 to help you consider which items might be taken into consideration when establishing the value of the Estate. Think of the 'Estate' as the figure you finally arrive at after adding up the values of all that you can reasonably identify and are required to declare by law (assets) then deducting any debts (liabilities).

You'll be introduced to the fundamental issues involved in the process and this book does its best to take you through stage by stage. It is usually not complicated and should hold no horrors for you.

Where you might come across complications in the particular set of circumstances with which you are dealing, the authors hope that you will be able to relate to one or more of the case histories that are included. These are all based on real situations and explain the solutions found at the time. None, of course, will be exactly the same as yours but they cover a variety of typical examples from the most simple to rather complex ones. If there isn't one that you can instantly identify with then various 'bits' from several others should guide you.

Enduring Powers of Attorney

Anyone can, if they so wish, give to another person the power to deal with their affairs through the appointment of that person under a formal Power of Attorney. These are now usually Enduring Powers of Attorney so as to ensure that the attorney still has power to deal with the 'Donor's' affairs even if the Donor becomes physically or mentally incapable. In these circumstances the attorney must register the Power at the Court of Protection and may not act under the Power until this has been done.

An Executor might come across this issue if the Testator has allowed them to know the contents of the Will when it is written and properly witnessed, often the case in close-knit family situations.

Any Executor needs to be aware that an Enduring Power of Attorney, and its authority, ceases at the death of the Donor of the Power. The Executors of the Will, under the powers and responsibilities they assume after the Testator's death, take over the administration of the Estate. If the Power has been registered at the Court of Protection, the Court must cancel the registration and will do so on production of a Death Certificate.

Living Wills

Much is talked and written about this subject these days; many emotions have been expressed – morally and emotionally. 'Living Wills' must be distinguished from Enduring Powers of Attorney, as, with the latter, the attorney's authority to deal with the Donor's property or financial affairs does not extend to health care decisions.

Even in family situations where a son, daughter or other close relative is also an Executor, it must be recognised that there is as yet no law to state the 'rules'. As already explained, Executors can only act after a death. The whole debate is beyond the scope and advice that this book can offer. Suffice it to say that, as in the section about Enduring Power of Attorney, this has no relevance to the Executors' responsibilities.

Domestic animals

As we have discussed above with regard to the need to find a Will quickly, it is also often the responsibility of an Executor to find a suitable home for any pet, of whatever size or shape, that the deceased may have had. Families or good neighbours might and often do help, but if none are available then you must find a rescue home to take care of them, at least in the short term to ensure they are fed properly. The latter are used to cries for help in such circumstances.

CASE HISTORY 1
'My Sister's Letter'

While remaining in contact with his family, Stuart had worked abroad all his working life. He told us what happened when his only sister, Moira, died suddenly:

'I was working on a contract in Oman when I received a cable from my sister's oldest friend, Jane, telling me that Moira had died suddenly and unexpectedly. I couldn't really believe it – she was younger than me after all – but nevertheless I caught the first plane I could find and headed for home to try to sort things out.

Our parents died when we were quite young, so I suppose it was inevitable that Moira and I were always very close. We had any number of aunts, uncles, cousins and so on, and were actually taken in by a maiden aunt, now long since passed away, but however good the rest of the family are in situations like this, they never can compensate for one's own parents. Moira and I made a pact when we were quite young that we would always look after each other, whatever happened, so you could say that ours was rather a special relationship.

Jane and I had arranged to meet at Moira's flat, and we spent a tearful evening while Jane told me what had happened.

Moira had always been employed in the health service and lived alone in her own flat just around the corner from the hospital where she worked. When she did not arrive at work that Monday morning, a colleague, receiving no answer to her telephone calls, grew anxious and contacted Jane, a mutual friend.

The two women met at Moira's flat but received no response when they rang and rang the doorbell. Upon looking through the letter box, Jane could just make out the figure of Moira lying on the floor in the hallway near the telephone. They lost no time in calling an ambulance and the police, who forced an entry. Tragically, Moira was beyond help and was pronounced dead. Of course, there had to be a post mortem to ascertain the cause of death, and it was concluded that Moira, always an asthmatic, had suffered from a serious attack which resulted in her death.

Poor Jane was in a terrible state. Apparently her phone had rung quite late the previous night and, since when she picked up the receiver she could hear nothing apart from a lot of 'heavy breathing', as she described it, she put the receiver down, thinking it was just another of the nuisance calls that plagued her from time to time. She had now convinced herself that it was Moira trying to get help and was utterly mortified.

I comforted Jane as best I could and she eventually seemed to recover a little. To my great surprise she produced a letter addressed to me in Moira's handwriting which she had been told to pass on to me in the event of my sister's death.

Now it was my turn to be tearful, and for Jane to comfort me. I can't describe what a joy it was to have such a personal reminder of Moira. In the letter she reminded me how, years before when I had landed a particularly lucrative contract, she had told me that I ought to write a Will leaving everything to her should I drop dead out in the wilderness somewhere. When I jokingly countered that in that case she too ought to make a Will she had laughed and said that she had nothing of any value to leave, so what was the point.

Unknown to me, she had thought about our conversation and had decided that while it wasn't really necessary to leave a 'proper Will', she had definite ideas about what should be done with her personal belongings, such as they were. In the letter she listed various items – a few pieces of relatively inexpensive jewellery, her books, her doll collection – and gave names and addresses of friends and relatives who might like to have them in the unlikely event of her death. I could almost hear Moira speaking when I read the final lines of the letter:

'There you go, Stu; I'm relying on you to do the necessary, just like you always promised you would – love you, Moira.'

I didn't really know where to start, but was told that once I had the death certificate I could visit the Registrar and make the funeral arrangements. So far, so good. Not knowing quite what to do next, I decided to visit the town's only solicitor and confidently produced Moira's letter. To my dismay, the solicitor said that while he thought it was really nice for me to have the letter, it really did not form a valid Will, since it was not witnessed, but it was perfectly all right for me to distribute the possessions Moira had spoken of since these were of only nominal value.

He advised me to give him as much detail as I possibly could of Moira's financial affairs, so I was eventually able to pass on details of bank and building society accounts, premium bonds, any unpaid bills and so on.

I remember I had to visit a Commissioner for Oaths to swear that I was Moira's only surviving close relative, and after that I left the whole thing to the solicitor and headed back to Oman. At his suggestion I agreed to him putting her flat on the market through a local estate agent. I think I only got one progress report and that was after about four months or so when I wrote to ask for some news.

The whole thing took seven or eight months, as I recall, but eventually Moira's flat was sold and I received the proceeds of the sale less quite a hefty sum in order to pay the solicitor – about £600 I think, which was a lot of money 15 years ago. I was in a good job, at the time, and wasn't really bothered too much about money, but by the time the mortgage on the flat had been paid off and the debts settled, there really wasn't much left over. If I hadn't been in the situation where I had to dash back to work it would probably have been wiser to deal with the whole matter myself.'

How could the matter have been better resolved?

Clearly, matters would have been simplified considerably had Moira made a proper Will. We have seen that Moira's letter to her brother was not regarded as a valid Will because it had not been witnessed. Too many people imagine that as long as they have made their wishes clear in writing, this is the end of the matter and they can be confident that their wishes will be carried out. In reality, of course, their effort and forethought is in vain if they do not think to get their signature on any such document properly witnessed.

In this case, the solicitor properly advised Stuart that he was at liberty to dispose of Moira's personal possessions according to her wishes as set down in the letter, since these were not seen as having any real monetary value. Indeed, the only item of monetary value possessed by Moira was the flat, on which she still had quite a large mortgage. By the time her building society had been paid off and the affair had dragged on for some months, quite a substantial amount was owing to the solicitor who had advised Stuart.

Obviously, Moira's death came as a great shock to Stuart, her loving brother. As soon as he received the bad news he rushed back from Oman without any clear idea of what one does when a close relative dies. In a state of turmoil and anxious to return to Oman, he rather hastily placed the matter in the hands of a solicitor rather than deal with it himself, no doubt seeing this as the 'easiest' solution.

Stuart, having no previous experience of such issues, assumed that only a solicitor could handle such matters. Despite the shock, and grief, following his sister's sudden death, his employers required him to return to his work in Oman as quickly as possible. However, in these days of effective worldwide communications, there is no reason why Stuart could not have set the wheels in motion himself and still returned to Oman to see the matter through at a distance. Even 15 years ago the telex and fax were in widespread use.

We have seen that Stuart actually did some of the work involved himself, assisted by Moira's good friend Jane. He had been able quickly and easily to work out Moira's financial situation and visited the Commissioner for Oaths to establish himself as Moira's closest relative. Rather than pass all this detail to a solicitor, despite having been frustrated by the fact that Moira's letter could not be regarded as a valid Will and Moira had thus died intestate, Stuart would have been well advised to apply for Letters of Administration and obtain permission to administer his sister's affairs himself.

After distributing those effects detailed in Moira's letter, Stuart stood to inherit his sister's other possessions, the flat being the only item of real value though heavily mortgaged.

He left the sale in the hands of the solicitor on his behalf, and it must be said that it was of course in the solicitor's best interests to sell the flat as quickly and painlessly as possible in order to wind up the Estate and realise his fee. With the best will in the world, it is unlikely that a solicitor, unless he were a personal friend, would go to enormous lengths to secure the best price possible when selling property on behalf of a client. The estate agent who handled the sale on the solicitor's instructions probably had no great motivation either as there was no pressure from the vendor, Stuart. This is not a particular criticism of either solicitor or estate agent, simply a fact of life.

Stuart, on the other hand, was perhaps too personally involved and, with the comfort zone of his high tax-free salary in the Middle East, saw no urgent need to sell the flat. In those days property prices were on a fairly dramatic upward spiral. Had Stuart dealt with the sale himself, even at a distance and probably through an estate agent he had appointed, it is possible that it might have sold for a larger sum. He, with more direct control, might have gained more from his sister's Estate. Of course solicitor's and estate agent's fees would have been charged on the sale of the property but there was no real need, in this case, for the substantial fees charged for managing a very simple administration.

CASE HISTORY 2
'The Family Rift'

David, a divorcee with custody of his only daughter, Susan, married a widow with two older children, Carole and Brian.

The new family lived together happily for many years. Carole, aged 18, married shortly after her mother's marriage to David, and Brian (13) and Susan (10) became as close as any natural brother and sister.

When David died prematurely after only 15 years of marriage to

Edna, he left all his possessions to her in a Will written shortly after they were married. Should Edna predecease him, Susan, Carole and Brian were to share everything. At that time Edna also wrote a Will making similar provisions for the three children, naming Brian as her Executor. David's brother, Richard, was named as his Executor and now takes up the tale:

> 'When David married Edna she was up to her eyes in debt. She had been struggling to pay a mortgage and was heavily in arrears, but David took over and soon got them on an even keel.
>
> Some years later he became unwell and was forced to take early retirement at 61. They had already moved to a smaller, newer house, mainly because David couldn't cope with the maintenance of the old one, nor the huge garden, but as his condition deteriorated, they bought a modern ground-floor flat with no garden. They had only been in the flat for a few months when David died, aged 63.
>
> I must admit I was a bit surprised when I found that the Will left everything to Edna. Since writing that Will, he and Edna had made quite a profit when they sold the old house and again on moving into the flat, and I'd have expected him to at least have left a sum of money to Susan – she was his only real daughter after all, and though he loved Edna's children, there's nothing like your own, is there? That would still have left Edna with the flat plus a few thousand in the bank. This is back in the early 1970s, of course, when the flat was valued at £15,000 and three or four thousand was considered a small fortune. Still, David's intentions were crystal clear and, as his Executor, it was my duty to swallow hard and administer the Estate according to his directions.'

Could the Executor have made a difference to the outcome?

In this case Richard, the Executor, carried out his duties efficiently and properly, whatever his personal feelings on the matter.

The Will was written some time prior to David's death, of course, long before he became ill and had to move house. We know that some profit was made buying and selling properties and it is just possible that David wrote a later Will which never came to light.

If Richard thought it so out of character that David had not made separate provision for his daughter Susan, perhaps he should have made more strenuous efforts to satisfy himself that the Will in his possession was indeed the *Last* Will, although even if a later Will had been unearthed, we have no guarantee that his wishes would have been in any way different from the wishes expressed in the earlier Will. We have only Richard's instinct to go on here.

It is most important that if an executor is appointed, he or she should make it his business to keep in touch with the person who appointed him to ensure that he knows the whereabouts of the Will and is kept informed if the Will is superseded by another at any time.

The Executor cannot influence the content, of course, and is not entitled to know the Testator's wishes until death. In this particular case, however, where the Executor is a very close friend or relative, it may well be that the Testator would have discussed the broad terms of the Will on an informal basis.

The Testator need not reveal the contents of his Will to anyone, of course, if he doesn't want to, but some people, especially if they are unwell at the time of making the Will, are only too glad for some impartial advice from a person they love and trust.

Subsequent events were to engender great feelings of bitterness in the other members of the family. Richard continues with the tale:

> 'Edna was in a state of shock, it was obvious, and naturally enough turned to her only daughter, Carole. She couldn't bear the thought of staying in the flat by herself so before any of us could blink, Carole had whisked her mother off to the coast for a two-week holiday for the two of them to give Edna 'breathing space'. Edna footed the bill for the holiday, of course.
>
> Carole and her husband, Frank, had a small shop, left by Frank's father many years before. It was in rather a scruffy area and they were living with their twins in the tiny two-bedroomed flat upstairs. She'd been nagging

Frank for years to buy a house but there was no way he could raise a sufficient loan on the basis of what he was making in the shop, even if they had managed to sell the flat. In any case, he was 20 years older than Carole and had been unable, so far, to get a mortgage on a larger property.

By the time they came back from their little holiday, Carole had talked Edna into selling the flat and 'lending' the proceeds to her so that she and Frank could add some money of their own and buy a property suitable for splitting into two self-contained flats. One flat would be for Carole and her family and the other for Edna. This was all a complete nonsense, of course, as Carole and Frank didn't have any money to put towards the purchase of a cardboard box, let alone a house. it was obvious to everyone that Edna would end up putting all the money into the venture herself while providing a new home for Carole, Frank and their children.

When Brian heard about it he was up in arms. He knew that on his mother's death her Estate was to be split equally between the three children, and even though Edna was still very much alive, Brian saw Carole as 'hijacking' his prospective inheritance in advance.

Carole tried to allay his fears, saying that Edna would be merely lending her the money; she and Frank would finance the building work necessary and she would own one of the flats, which would represent her advance share of the eventual inheritance. Edna would live in the other flat until she died, when her flat would be sold on the open market and Brian and Susan would share the proceeds.

It all sounded very plausible, but Brian was suspicious, knowing the way his sister's mind worked, and talked it over with Susan, whom he felt he could trust. Susan was disappointed, of course, that her father had not left her any money, but her attitude was to shrug her shoulders and accept that if her father had left all his money to Edna then so be it. The money was Edna's to do with as she wished. Even if Edna decided to make a new Will leaving everything to her own two children, Carole and Brian, there would be nothing Susan could do about it.

I could scream at Susan sometimes; she can be so pigheaded. She was entitled to something rather than let Carole scoop the pool, but she wouldn't listen, just went on about it all being an undignified scramble for money made even more tasteless because Edna hadn't actually died yet!

However, Brian was a different character altogether, and simply wouldn't leave it alone. Eventually he nagged poor old Edna into signing a piece of paper which stated that she had sold the flat for £15,000 and that this money had been lent to Carole in order to buy a suitable property which would be converted into two flats. In the event of Edna's death, one of the flats was to be sold and the money shared between Brian and Susan. If she died before the flats had been built, Carole would already have had her one-third share of the property, and Brian and Susan would each receive one-third of the eventual selling price of the property. This seemed to satisfy Brian – for the time being – though it didn't exactly improve relations between Carole and Brian, as you can imagine, especially as Brian insisted on the document being properly witnessed, just like a Will. Brother and sister were scarcely on speaking terms after that.

With the proceeds from Edna's flat, Carole and Frank bought a three-bedroomed house just around the corner from their shop and moved in, letting their old flat. They moved Edna into the upstairs of the house, even though it would have made much more sense for a woman of her years to live on the ground floor, where she wouldn't have to cope with stairs as she grew older.

Edna had a few thousand in the bank when she moved in, and Carole and Frank spent most of it extending downstairs in order to provide themselves with spacious living accommodation, and converting the box bedroom into a kitchen for Edna. Then they claimed they had run out of money, but not before they treated themselves to completely new furniture as all their old furniture had been left in their flat for their tenant, who was paying them a reasonable rent for furnished accommodation.

Brian, of course, was now furious. His biggest cause for concern was not just that Carole had managed to wheedle so much money out of their mother, but there was now no chance of any more money being spent in order to make the two flats completely independent of each other; all the money had gone and Edna was no more than a lodger in her daughter's home, and a not particularly comfortable lodger at that.

She was a good bit older than David, and with failing health became a virtual prisoner in the upstairs of that house, relying on Carole increasingly for shopping and so on. Edna had a lonely life, really, though Brian used to visit her from time to time, carefully avoiding his sister with whom he by now found it almost impossible to have a civilized conversation.

The shock of David's death had left Edna in poor health, and I dare say that when her devoted daughter entered into all this she wasn't expecting her mother to last as long as she did. Towards the end she wasn't a particularly easy old lady, quite cantankerous in fact, and according to Brian, and much to his sly amusement, she took a perverse pleasure in having Carole hopping up and down the stairs every five minutes at her beck and call. Apparently they tried to persuade her to move into an old people's home but she wouldn't have it – said it would cost *them* too much money; that soon shut them up. They even tried to get Brian and his wife to take Edna on, but he laughed in their faces – said they'd made their bed and now they could lie in it.

Frank retired some years ago, a semi-invalid, so Carole had her work cut out trying to run the shop and look after him and her mother. There was no sympathy from Brian.

At the age of 85, Edna passed away peacefully in her sleep. It was the start of open unpleasantness.

Brian, of course, leapt into the fray with almost indecent haste. Flourishing his mother's Will and the letter she had written so many years ago, he coldly informed his sister that she had no choice but to sell the property so that he and Susan could receive their rightful inheritance.

Carole tried to tell Brian that the letter was not valid, and that he and Susan should consider themselves lucky to get £5,000 each from the original sale of David and Edna's old flat. Besides, she continued, she had had the burden of looking after Edna for many years and surely deserved some recompense for that.

Completely unmoved, Brian insisted that the letter served as a Codicil to the Will and was perfectly valid as it had been signed and witnessed properly. Carole was aghast, and after some weeks of heated argument was persuaded to take Brian's word for it rather than engage the expensive services of a solicitor. After all, Brian had been quietly fuming over the whole affair for many years and had had plenty of time in recent years to establish the legal position.

I was a bit surprised that she took Brian's word for it, but she was obviously worn out with looking after Frank and her mother, not to mention trying without success to hang onto an ailing business, which had gone severely downhill since Frank retired. The shop had been standing empty for some months, and they had not yet found anyone willing to rent it from them. No, Carole just wanted an end to the whole affair; I was beginning to feel almost sorry for her by this time.

Carole couldn't face the prospect of moving back into the flat, and I gather that eventually it was agreed that she and Frank would sell the flat above the shop and with some of the proceeds long-delayed building work would finally take place in order to provide the two independent flats originally envisaged.

The building work seemed to take for ever, and after many months of wrangling between brother and sister, it was eventually agreed that in recognition of Carole and Frank looking after Edna for so many years, they would remain in the larger, ground-floor flat as their slightly larger portion of the original legacy, and the one-bedroom upstairs flat upstairs would be sold and the proceeds shared between Brian and Susan.

As far as I know, that was the end of the story. I personally lost all touch with the family after that, apart from Susan, of course.'

Could the Executor have made better arrangements for the beneficiaries in this case?

First of all, we should say that Brian was quite right in stating that the piece of paper Edna signed and had witnessed was *probably* perfectly valid in the eyes of the law. According to the Wills Act of 1837, a Will is revoked (wholly or partially) by a later Will or Codicil or 'by some writing declaring an intention to revoke the same and executed in the manner of a Will'. However, there are potential dangers here. Anyone wishing to challenge could question the 'piece of paper', claiming that it was inadequate and not intended as a Will. It could also be claimed that Brian, as a beneficiary, might have exercised 'undue influence' on Edna in her weakened state of health, and possibly mind. The point made earlier about the desirability of rewriting a Will, rather than having Codicils or 'pieces of paper', however properly witnessed, becomes obvious. There is far less opportunity for the Last Will to be challenged if it has been formally written and the Testator's signature properly witnessed.

In order to discover whether Brian could have made arrange-ments which would have advantaged the beneficiaries further, we needed to know the actual sums of money involved, and Richard put us in touch with Brian, who agreed to reveal the details.

Apparently, Carole and Frank had had a succession of undesirable tenants in their flat above the shop and it was in a poor state of repair to say the least. Situated in rather an unattractive area and with an empty, vandalized shop beneath, they considered themselves lucky to eventually sell it leasehold for £25,000. Approximately £10,000 of this sum was spent on building work necessary to properly convert the house into two flats, and the upstairs flat was eventually sold for £30,000. Brian and Susan thus received £15,000 each while Carole retained the ground floor flat, valued at £38,000, the £15,000 or so left over from the sale of their original flat above the shop, and of course the shop itself, albeit in extremely poor condition.

Even after all this time, Brian was still exceedingly bitter over the whole affair, claiming that Carole had, once again, ended up 'on top' in financial terms. We gently pointed out that it should not be forgotten that Carole and Frank did own the shop with the flat above in the first place, and Carole had looked after Edna for a number of years, at which he appeared slightly mollified.

With help from local property agents, we established that the street in which the shop and flat were situated had become extremely run down following the development of a brand new shopping mall nearby. One by one the shops had emptied and now stood derelict or were being sold off for residential redevelopment.

Furthermore, we were advised that had the house been sold at the time of Edna's death, it would probably have fetched about £60,000 had it been marketed as being 'ripe for development into two self-contained flats'. Each of the three beneficiaries would then have obtained £20,000, £5,000 more than they had actually received.

Carole and Frank, whose children by this time had grown up and left home, could have moved back into the flat with £20,000 in the bank. This would seem at first sight to be a fair solution, since they would then be placed in exactly the position they were in before the deaths of Edna and David, except that they would have a legacy of £20,000 – exactly the same as their co-beneficiaries. They could even have eventually sold the shop and flat for residential development and added their £20,000 in order to purchase a new property for themselves.

However, as a matter of interest, we investigated whether there could have been an even 'better' outcome, particularly from Carole's point of view, since we already know that she was emotionally opposed to returning to the flat and would probably never have listened to the suggestions put in the above paragraph. Furthermore, according to Brian, she was fixated on the idea that she should receive some recompense for having cared for Edna for so many years.

Had Brian and Carole been able to discuss the matter more

rationally, it seems that an ideal solution might have been for Carole to 'buy' Susan and Brian out of the whole property. We have seen that she sold the flat above the shop for £25,000 and was left with an empty shop which she had been unable to let and it was deteriorating rapidly. How much more sensible it would have been had she and Frank sold the whole premises. We found that other properties in the street had successfully been sold with residential planning permission, and our property developer gives us reason to suppose that Carole and Frank could have sold the whole property for around £70,000.

We have seen that the house was valued at £60,000 at the time of Edna's death, so Carole could have purchased it herself from the sale of the shop/flat premises and Brian and Susan could have received their shares of £20,000 each.

In this manner, Brian and Susan would have received £20,000 each and Carole, with a husband whose health was failing, would not have had the upset of having to move out of the home she always wanted. If she so wished, she could have moved lodgers into Edna's old accommodation upstairs, where she could keep an eye on them, thus providing a small extra income and of course she would still have £10,000 or so in the bank.

Had Brian persuaded the other beneficiaries to take the latter course of action, the whole matter could have been resolved more quickly, rather than waiting months for building work to be completed and for the sale of Edna's old flat to take place, during which the relationship between brother and sister deteriorated massively.

2

Getting Started

Where do I start?

As soon as someone dies having left a valid Will, it is immediately effective. The Executor's powers to act start at the moment of death despite the fact that it is going to take some time to prove the Will formally according to the laws that apply. The ultimate granting of probate simply becomes an official confirmation of the powers that the Executor has had and exercised since the death of the Testator.

Much will depend here, for the Executor, on the nature of his or her relationship with the deceased and family.

When someone dies there are a number of procedures that have to be followed prior to a funeral, burial or cremation. This applies equally to the release of a body or any of its organs for the pursuit of medical science in whatever manner was wished by the deceased, or could in certain circumstances be decided by close relatives, or Executors, soon after the death.

These procedures are statutory and are in no way related to whether or not there is a Will. If you are a close relative or friend of someone who has died intestate, the advice that follows will be helpful anyway.

The death certificate is the first and most important document that is needed and without it nothing can be progressed. If death occurs in a hospital a doctor will sign the appropriate *initial medical death certificate*, as will a general practitioner for a death at home.

If the death is sudden and unexpected and a doctor is not immediately available it is usual for the body to be removed for autopsy, as happened in Case History 1 at the end of Chapter 1.

Here an initial death certificate is issued after the autopsy has been carried out. Whatever the circumstances, the certificate is available for the nearest relative or an Executor.

This can be a more complex procedure – for example if the circumstances tragically involve murder or suicide or death in what the police officially describe as 'suspicious circumstances'. Matters are not so simple, either, when someone dies abroad and you want the body returned for burial. There are special procedures that apply for serving members of the Armed Forces. In Scottish law there are, again, different procedures.

We shall not go into these in detail at this point, but if you find that in your case one of these applies then read Appendix 2 now. There you will find comprehensive advice on what to do and where to get necessary help. Return then to this point of the book because most of what follows will probably still apply in some way.

What do I do with the death certificate?

The initial medical death certificate then has to be delivered to the Registrar of Births, Deaths and Marriages who must have this document within five days of the date of death. It can be sent in the post but a personal visit is strongly recommended.

Generally the Registry is most helpful, though we have heard stories of their offices being undermanned in certain towns, leading to frustrating waiting times. Let's hope that you'll be more lucky, but do set aside plenty of time in case you are not. You are dealing with sadness and trauma; to them it is their job and they are sensitive to human emotions.

Only the Registrar can issue the formal and official death certificate which is then going to become very important to you, the Executor, in the forthcoming weeks and even months.

Make sure you get extra certified copies!

When you visit the Registrar, you'll probably be inundated with leaflets to help guide you and offer practical advice on issues that may be worrying you. The Registrar might even be able to point out something that you need to do in the early stages which in the drama of the moment you could easily overlook, and regret having done so later.

Although you will be charged a nominal sum, it is recommended that you obtain extra certified copies of the Death Certificate whilst visiting the Registrar, even when dealing with a seemingly uncomplicated Estate. You will find that you will need them; the more complex the Estate, the more you will need. When attempting to release the deceased's assets – for example, property, contents of bank accounts, etc – you will obviously have to prove not only that the owner of the asset has indeed died but that you have been appointed Executor.

Since mere photocopies of the Death Certificate are often not acceptable, you will save a great deal of time and frustration by obtaining more certified copies than you feel you need, rather than being forced to wait for a precious certified copy to be returned from one organization before you can send it to another.

More about Probate

One leaflet which should be offered will be form PA2, entitled *How to obtain probate*. If this is not offered, do ask for one, since it explains *how* and *where* to apply for a Grant of Probate, and *who* can apply. Get one at an early stage in the process of undertaking your duties as an Executor. It is short and written very straightforwardly. Like this book, it is designed for those who have from the outset decided not to employ solicitors.

A *Grant of Probate* is in effect a court order, leading to a document bearing the court seal, which constitutes the Executor's legal proof of entitlement to administer the deceased's Estate. Without such a grant, some organizations will not release assets held in the deceased's name. The Executor is thus rendered powerless to get on with the job in hand.

There are circumstances, of course, where a Grant of Probate or Letters of Administration are not always necessary – for instance, if the assets amount to less than £5,000 currently, or if all property was jointly owned and the mortgage paid off. The asset holder, at their discretion, may pay out without a Grant of Probate. The best way to find out is to ask the asset holder if they require Probate. This may save a lot of unnecessary time and costs. This was the situation in Case History 6 at the end of Chapter 5.

Like the Registrar of Births, Deaths and Marriages, the *Probate Registry* (or Commissary Office, in Scotland) is accustomed to guiding executors through the seemingly daunting maze of paperwork. You should therefore waste no time in contacting your local Probate Registry. This can most easily be done by simply looking them up in the telephone directory.

On request, the Probate Registry will send you various forms to be completed. It can sometimes take two or three weeks to obtain these forms, so...

Be patient with the bureaucrats!

We all know that paperwork is boring but some is vital, cannot be avoided and is often the only passport that will allow you to take the next step forward. You will doubtless find that some of the people whose life is spent dealing with it are themselves pedantic and may occasionally appear inhumane in the context in which you will be dealing with them. They are only interested in getting it absolutely correct, and usually then only in timescales appropriate to them. Play by their rules as best you can and you should not have many problems.

If you think that the authors are being cynical then you are right. We are just making you aware of some of the things that so many who have contributed to this book have been through. Cynical we may be, but negative, no! If you can gain their confidence, often with flattery, you might be able to move things along more quickly on compassionate grounds.

In reality, most of the people that you are likely to be in contact with in the early stages are very empathetic and sympathetic; in the case of some undertakers, even sycophantic. It is more likely that you will find the frustrations later in the administration process. Hopefully you will not, but it is suggested that you keep an open mind, and especially a sense of humour, for some of the bureaucracy that you may experience.

Our experiences with Probate and Land Registries, and even that perceived ogre the Inland Revenue, have generally been most helpful and friendly. Sadly, it has been in dealings among the private commercial sector with banks, insurance companies, company share registration departments and the like that the greatest frustrations have at times been found.

In most aspects of our daily lives *courtesy* brings its rewards. A simple cry like 'Please, can you help me, I've never had to do this before?' will usually not only gain the help you may require but also save a great deal of your time and needless frustration. Most of those employed in public service do believe they are there to serve and take a pride in doing so. They also, as we all do, *respond warmly to the 'please' and 'thank you' approach* too often lacking in today's society.

... but what about those wretched forms?

This book shows you what some look like, how you can handle them, and how to work with the people who deal with them and on whom you are going to rely for speedy processing. We explain where to go to get them and where you will get advice on processing them. The Probate Registry, the Inland Revenue and the Land Registry all have well-written, plain English leaflets or booklets with which they can provide you. They are usually pleased to assist you in completing them correctly.

You as an Executor may be at arm's length from this immediacy. Perhaps someone closer wants to do this all this and arrange the funeral. In this case you will not want to be seen to be interfering at such a time. You should, though, try to be aware and satisfied that others are doing the right thing according to the wishes of the deceased as you understand them at this early stage. It is important that funeral costs should not be out of proportion to the likely value of the assets of the deceased's Estate.

Can certain wishes be overridden?

As an Executor you will want to maximize the value of the Estate and do in certain instances have the power to override any impractical wishes that the deceased might have specified – and one hears of some bizarre requests. A wish to have a body, or even ashes, sent to the USA on Concorde and then transported to an obscure part of the Arizona Desert for interment might reasonably be considered impractical or, more probably, simply not affordable unless the value of the Estate was immense. If there is that sort of money there is a chance that the request was from someone whose eccentricities were well-known to you and that separate provision had been made.

There are other ways in which the wishes expressed in a Will can be overridden. The great Charles Dickens left at his death in 1870 a Will stating 'on no account make me the subject of any monument, memorial or testimonial whatever'. Subsequent generations of direct descendants and a society dedicated to the study of his works believe that he never really meant this and that it was written tongue-in-cheek. For some years his image has adorned the reverse of our £10 banknotes. Since the first edition of this book the effigy of Dickens has yet to materialize in the UK. However, the City of Portsmouth (UK) has a Charles Dickens Museum in its care. There is an effigy in Philadelphia, USA.

In Case History 3, at the end of this chapter, you will read how the Testator's wishes could have been amended for the greater good of the named beneficiaries.

Technically, the Executors are entitled to possession of the deceased's body where a Will has been made. If the next of kin is not an Executor then you will in most cases naturally need to consult immediately with the next of kin as well as beneficiaries. Usually everyone will want the body disposed of without undue delay and with dignity. You also will want this to be done with appropriate cost-effectiveness and must use your judgement and common sense, but the authority to do as you wish is yours. Any directions regarding disposal that might have been written into a Will are not mandatory. If there is no Will then the responsibility for the body and its disposal falls to the next of kin.

The body and the medical profession

Often nowadays people wish to leave their body, or certain organs, either for the purpose of trying to save the life of another or to be used for medical research. Arrangements for this may or may not have been made with appropriate medical authorities. The next of kin, or Executor, may not have been made aware of this. In cases where this issue has never been raised in the past then the Executor has absolute discretion should the medical authorities request permission to examine the body or use parts of it *unless* the deceased either in writing, or even in conversation, had expressly stated in front of two witnesses that this was not to happen under any circumstances. Also a spouse or very close relative can reasonably object to the body being interfered with in any way. The Anatomy Act of 1832 is still on the statute books and there is also a Human Tissue Act 1961 which covers this matter should you ever need to have recourse to them.

It can be a sensitive and sometimes delicate issue for Executors to have to handle. If the matter is left to you then you will want to discuss it with the spouse and/or next of kin and endeavour to comply with their wishes if appropriate.

Don't panic!

In Chapter 1 the importance of finding the Will as soon as possible after death was mentioned a number of times and in a number of contexts. Usually, though, the focus is, and should be, on making the appropriate funeral arrangements quickly and, quite simply and without any disrespect, 'getting it over with'.

After this is done and people begin to reorganize their everyday lives, often with the pain of having lost a loved one, there usually is plenty of time to plan the sorting out of the deceased's affairs and to work through Probate, Administration and the ultimate distribution of any funds or effects designated in the Will.

First-time Executors often charge around in a rush, unsure of themselves, having been thrust into an environment of which they have no previous experience. The secret to ensuring that all will progress in an orderly way is not to panic.

Initially you must just take time and *think*:

- What are the main issues likely to be involved?
- What apparent assets are there and where are they?
- Might there be other assets?

- What liabilities can be established?
- Who are the beneficiaries?
- Where are the beneficiaries?
- Might there be people excluded who believe they have a claim on the Estate?
- What taxation implications are probable or possible?
- Anything else you can think of that might be relevant!

So what next?

The forms winging their way from the Probate Registry will demand a great deal of financial detail regarding the deceased's Estate, so now is the time to ensure you are adequately prepared. If exact figures can not be given at this stage, realistic estimates are acceptable to the Probate Registry.

First protect the assets

This is the perhaps the one aspect of Administration where you may have to move quickly to protect the value of the deceased's Estate.

Having obtained copies of the official death certificate, you must act as quickly as you reasonably can to ensure that all the assets of the deceased are established and secured. Case History 6 at the end of Chapter 5 gives an example of the importance of securing even apparently trivial assets.

The most urgent administrative actions to be taken are to inform:

- bank, building society and post office accounts;
- employers or, if retired, the pension fund or insurance company paying the pension;
- Department of Social Security if a pension or a benefit of any kind is being paid – any overpayment made will be clawed back later and this can be very distressing;
- insurance companies – check for all the possible policies there may be: personal, car, household, mortgage, health care and whatever. Fully secure the dwelling should it now be empty in accordance with the requirements of the houseowner's and householder's insurance policies. Advise the insurance

company or companies of the situation, the actions that the Executors will be taking, and take whatever advice they may offer into account;

- any financial adviser the deceased may have had or other agent with whom they consulted;
- HM Inspector of Taxes;
- are there Premium Bonds, stocks or shares, loans to private individuals or companies etc;
- the DSS regarding loans of medical equipment – which could include anything such as a wheelchair, walking frame or any household aid. It might sound gruesome but heart pacemakers should be returned (and anyway must be removed prior to a cremation). Prescribed medication should be returned to the doctor for disposal;
- the Royal Mail to redirect post! Most will be 'junk mail' and you will easily recognise those envelopes that might be important to the administration process. This is one of the most distressing aspects for the survivor to be constantly reminded of a lost loved one by this kind of computer produced rubbish. An effective way is to return it unopened with a large scribble in a bright-coloured highlighter pen stating 'dead'. It usually stops the flow and helps reduce the upset.

Why so important so soon?

Imagine a situation where a husband dies and his widow and perhaps other family living at home have been solely or largely dependent on his income, *or* there is the death of a single man or woman who was the sole provider of the income needed to bring up children or to look after an aged or handicapped person.

In this situation, all bank, building society, post office savings, credit cards and other accounts in a single name are automatically frozen at death and cannot be accessed. Where is the next meal coming from, let alone money for rent, mortgage payments, rates and any outstanding bills for electricity, gas or the telephone (which will suddenly be more heavily used than usual)?

Sadly these situations and variants occur every day throughout the land unless a supply of cash is kept readily available in the home – something we are all advised against.

People planning for death and afterwards will write a Will which makes good financial provision for the future of their survivors in the long term. All too often the immediate financial implications that can result from death are overlooked. Apart from the sadness and emotion, the bereaved are also thrown into the awful and highly disturbing situation where, however secure their longer-term futures may be, they literally don't know where the next penny is coming from for their everyday lives and immediate expenses which, in the circumstances, will be greater than usual.

Where this is the case the Probate Registry will do all they can to issue a Grant of Probate as quickly as possible. Make all the circumstances known as soon as possible and preferably to a manager.

Where there has been a joint account – and presuming there are funds in it – then obviously there will be access to those funds, but they might be strictly limited.

If you want no involvement

If an appointed Executor does not want to be involved, he or she must not interfere with the assets other than to protect them.

Should you decide that, for whatever reason, you cannot undertake the role of Executor then you must contact the nearest or an appropriate Probate Registry. They will provide you with a formal document known as a letter of renunciation for you to sign and have your signature formally witnessed. It is a formality and you are not obliged to give a reason.

If you already have the Will in your possession the Registry will advise you. Should you know of no one who might act in your place you can hand over the Will to them and get a receipt. Your involvement is then over.

If the Executors decline to act, it is usual for the Grant to be issued to the chief beneficiary named in the Will. In these circumstances the Grant is called a Grant of Letters of Administration with Will annexed.

What if there is no Will – Intestacy

If there is no Will to be found, or there is one but it is deemed invalid for whatever reason, then the deceased is said to have died Intestate. Under the Administration of Estates Act 1925 the personal representative of the deceased (now referred to as an Administrator) has to adopt very similar procedures to those an Executor (as formally appointed in a Will) would follow. This is what *should* have happened in Case History 4 at the end of this chapter.

With the knowledge that the deceased was solvent, and their Estate above the value of £5,000 in England and Wales (£17,000 in Scotland), then application to the Probate Registry has to be made. In the case of Intestacy the application is for a Grant of Letters of Administration, and where there is a valid Will the Executor applies for a Grant of Probate.

Intestacy can be a much longer process for the Administrator to wind up an Estate – years rather than months in many cases. Where there is a Will, the Executor can move much more rapidly and effectively to distribute the Estate.

It is understood that there are more women disadvantaged as a result of Intestacy than divorce. Currently some 40 per cent of marriages end in divorce – a disturbing statistic. As a general rule women live longer than men and are therefore more likely to be the ones who are left with the difficulties. As one lawyer defined Intestacy, 'It is the legal definition for someone being left in a mess just because their husband or wife couldn't be bothered, or were too penny-pinching, to make a Will.'

Intestacy rules

As indicated above, these can be complex especially where a death or divorce has taken place and where there are offspring from remarriages.

While this book is primarily designed to help the formally appointed Executor in their task you will find, in Chapter 8, some guidelines for the Administrator in cases of Intestacy and Partial Intestacy.

CASE HISTORY 3
'The Animal Lover'

Executors' lack of imagination or neglect of duty?

This case is one where the Executors followed the wording of the Will in every detail, acting exactly according to the wishes of the deceased. In this case it would have been better if some more imagination had been used and the mechanisms of the law brought into play. This would have been to the advantage of the two main parties named as beneficiaries.

Some stories have a bizarre sting in the tail. The following is one of missed opportunities for the beneficiaries, and is related here by a friend of the deceased.

'I couldn't call myself a friend of the late Mrs Finch, really she didn't have many friends – but I certainly knew her better than most – all my life in fact.

She came from a very good old family who were wealthy landowners around here, so she was considered quite a catch, as we used to say. We all thought she'd end up as an old maid, to tell you the truth, in spite of her money – she was a difficult woman even then – but to everyone's surprise at the age of 47 she married a good-looking young local man 15 years her junior. Her parents bought them a lovely little house in the village with a fair bit of land.

Mr Finch never really lived up to her expectations and she was forever reminding him of it, and in public too. Why he stuck by her I'll never know – I suppose it was the money – but stick by her he did. Wouldn't hear a word against her either; a lovely man, real gentleman.

Of course, that house wasn't good enough for Mary Finch, and after a few years she sold it to property developers, who razed it to the ground and threw up a load of dreadful, ugly houses on the site. Her name was mud in the village after that, I can tell you.

Not that she cared. She bought the Old Rectory and proceeded to live in the style she had been used to as a girl, with servants and all that nonsense. In this day and age? There was a man to do the gardening, a cook, if you don't mind, and a cleaning lady – not that any one of them stayed with her for long – she was that difficult to please. Poor Mr Finch was treated like the hired help by all accounts, and used to keep out of the way as much as he could – working all day at the local cheese factory and spending many of his evenings at the Swan enjoying the darts and skittles and so on.

We could all see that she couldn't possibly keep all this up on Mr Finch's wages. Everyone assumed that she had made a killing when she sold the property to the developers and of course when her parents died, as the only child she would also have inherited some money – we thought lots – but you can never know, can you?

They never did have any children, of course, since, let's face it, she was a bit past childbearing age by the time they got married, and I reckon that this was probably the start of her obsession with animals. Some sort of substitute. It started with the odd stray cat and dog, until before you could say Jack Robinson she'd got a right menagerie up there.

By this time, no one would work for the woman. Mind you, my Ron used to go and do a bit of gardening and odd-jobbing here and there, but only for Mr Finch's sake, otherwise he'd have been trying to do it all, on top of his job. Obviously, there was no real need for him to carry on working, but I dare say he was glad to get out of the house each day, and they were a good bunch at the cheese factory.

Sheila Jackson used to go up there once a week and tidy round for them, more out of loyalty than anything, but even she got fed up with it in the end and handed in her notice. 'Place reeks of cat pee,' she used to say. 'Fair turns your stomach, it does.' She reckoned that at one time there were 14 cats, breeding all over the place. Mary Finch didn't believe in having them doctored. Six or seven dogs, hens, an old lame donkey, a couple of pigs and whatever else besides. 'More like Noah's ark, up there,' she used to say, 'Noah's bloody ark.'

Well, they plodded along like that for years. Mr Finch

was never what you'd call a strong man and his health gave out eventually. He took early retirement, not that he'd have got more than a pittance from the factory. This meant of course he was thrown into her company full-time.

She raised hell, apparently, called him all the lazy layabouts and spongers under the sun. He, of course, reacted by spending more and more time propping up the bar at the Swan while she threw herself into looking after her wretched private zoo.

Oh, she was a worker all right, I'll give her that. She was up with the lark feeding and grooming those smelly creatures of hers, and though the house was a tip those animals' quarters were spotless. If I'd been Mr Finch I think I'd have been tempted to move in with the pigs; I'm sure he would have been a damned sight more comfortable!

Then one day Mr Finch went to the Swan and had rather more than his usual, which was quite a lot, but he could cope with it and never made a fool of himself or a scene. Had to be taken home, he did. Not like him at all, we all thought; something must have happened. Well it had; apparently Mrs Finch had had a massive heart attack and went, just like that. Mr Finch was utterly bewildered by the whole thing and didn't really seem to be able to grasp it at first. He didn't seem exactly grief-stricken, but nor did he seem pleased she'd gone and he was free at last.

He never said a word against her, even when slightly in his cups, but plodded on, doing for himself and asking no favours of anyone. The animals were all taken off to an animal sanctuary somewhere, apart from Mr Finch's favourite two old cats which only lived on for another year or so. I really think he was quite sorry, in a funny sort of way, to see all the others go.

We all thought he'd waste no time putting the old house on the market. I mean, what was the point in him rattling round in a great big place like that? It would have been much better for him to sell up and buy himself a little sheltered flat in the village. But he didn't. He stayed put, and eventually the word got round that in her Will, Mrs Finch had left virtually all she had – everything including the house – to the animal sanctuary that took her own animals when she died.

Apparently there was a bit in a bank account to pay for the funeral costs and we gathered she left £1,000 or more to the favoured cousin named as an executor, and £2,000 to the animal sanctuary specifically nominated to care for her animals so long as they took them in. It seems that was it. Mr Finch didn't get a penny to bless himself, poor thing, but *was* allowed to live in the house, fully furnished, for as long as he lived. Once he died, the animal sanctuary could sell the house and take the proceeds. The great wealth that us locals imagined must have been there simply did not exist.

Steadily the Old Rectory deteriorated. Mr Finch didn't have the money to keep it up and it has been pitiful to see that fine old building crumbling round his ears.

He's still hanging on – living in just one room and the kitchen, since he can't afford to heat the rest. There are a few pieces of quite valuable furniture, but of course if he were to sell it it would become the property of the animal sanctuary, so there it sits, being eaten alive by wood-worm and the old man can't afford to keep himself warm. I'd have had the lot on the back of the fire by now rather than let them have it.

Me and Sheila Jackson like to keep a bit of an eye on him, getting him the odd bit of shopping – that sort of thing – but he's a proud man and won't accept any other kind of help. He still trots down to the Swan quite regular, but his legs are beginning to go now, and, of course, he hasn't got the money he once had. The regulars would stand him all the odd half pints and whisky tots he could drink these days, but as I say, he's a proud man and insists on his independence.

It's not right that he should be living like that. The Social call in, and he gets meals on wheels and a lady to attend to his feet and that, but he just digs his heels in when offered a place in an old people's home. 'I've got my own home,' he smiles. 'Besides, I've got this cat of my own now and I wouldn't be allowed to take him into one of those places.'

I reckon the day he leaves that house it'll be feet-first, in his box. I'd love to know what goes on in his head. Maybe he actually did think something of old Mary Finch and wants to stay in the house with his memories, who can tell? Personally, I think it more likely he's hanging on out of spite. You know, 'she didn't leave me a penny, left it all to that damned animal sanctuary, so I'm going to bide my time, let them wait for it', that sort of thing.

By the time they get their hands on it, it won't be worth having – apart from the value of the land it stands on, of course. Mind you, that place is a listed building so they'll not get permission to develop it. Whoever buys it will have to spend loads to get it back together, probably do a nice job on it. It'll sell real cheap.'

What a sad tale. With little more than village gossip to go on, we shall never know how Mr Finch's problems might have been avoided.

His story is told merely to illustrate the kind of problems left behind for the living, and there is little doubt that stories like this are to be found in towns and villages all over the land.

There was clearly potentially quite a lot of money at stake here. Mr Finch could have contested the will on the basis of its unfairness, and on the grounds that his late wife grew more and more eccentric in her old age; the Will might even be found invalid. While this might have been possible, and it probably would not have taken a great deal of money to argue through the courts, in reality Mr Finch did not have the money to employ legal advice in the first place and Legal Aid would have been an unlikely proposition.

Application could have been made under the Inheritance (Provision for Family and Dependants) Act 1975. The court would then have to apply the relevant standards under the Act in deciding what provision might be made. However, the court's decision is entirely discretionary after it has given consideration to guidelines such as the size of the Estate, the financial resources and earning capacity of the applicant and the obligations of the deceased towards the applicant.

In reality, the better approach would probably have been for Mr Finch, through the Executors, to have come to an agreement with the animal charity to vary the Will so as to allow him to sell the Old Rectory, move into a small house, and use some of the money to provide an income during his life. It is possible to vary the terms of a Will up to two years after the death of the Testator as long as all the beneficiaries agree. Hence the capital sum to be taken ultimately by the charity would be preserved while allowing Mr Finch a better standard of living and quality of life.

Did Mr Finch know about his wife's plans before she died? It is unlikely that she ever mentioned them, except possibly as a threat which he never took seriously. Even if he had thought about such a possibility, could he have persuaded her to amend her Will in order that he could care for himself more adequately in his old age? My conversations with the lovely old man suggest that such communication could never have happened: 'I could never be the boss, see, not with her. She were older, and probably wiser, so she kept saying.' He just wanted a quiet life and had it well organized on his terms. There were few rows and he wanted to keep it that way; hence separate lives. He had never contemplated the consequences of her dying before him despite the age difference. She did! Mr Finch is now in his late 80s.

After Mrs Finch's death

At least under the terms of Mrs Finch's Will the old man was allowed to remain in the house, but her beloved animal sanctuary is still waiting to realise the rest of its inheritance. Had Mrs Finch been better advised at the time of making her Will, or at the very least discussed it with her husband, she might have made more realistic provision for both Mr Finch and the animal sanctuary. We know too little of the real nature of their relationship to speculate further on this issue. That aspect of the affair remains a mystery.

Seemingly Mr Finch sat back and accepted his wife's wishes. Was this because he was a simple man who didn't know he could have contested the Will, or an old-fashioned, honourable one who believed her wishes should be fulfilled at whatever cost to himself?

Even if Mr Finch had contested the Will and obtained the major share of her property, who is to know whether he might have chosen to stay on in the house anyway, with his memories. I did not seek to put any of these questions to Mr Finch. At 88 years of age, it seemed kinder to leave him in peace.

The Executors
Mrs Finch had named the old faithful family solicitor (and family friend), together with a cousin of hers, the same age as her 'young' husband, as joint Executors. Given the nature of the marriage and the source of the money that was once hers, it seems unlikely that she would even have contemplated the involvement of her much younger husband in 'family matters'.

The Executors could have avoided this no-win situation for the beneficiaries of this slightly bizarre but not unusual Will. They did not. Even the solicitor had not the imagination to do more than the minimum in exercising his duties as an Executor; the cousin was scarcely versed in such matters and was happy to be guided. One has to assume that the strategy of doing nothing relied on an assumption that Mr Finch would not live so long as he has. Also, property was a secure and forever appreciating asset, they probably thought. Neither Executor cared much for animals anyway.

The consequences
Highly respected in the village for his gentle, uncomplaining nature, 88-year-old widower Mr Finch continues to live in squalor in a gradually disintegrating property. No family has come forward to offer more suitable accommodation and it would appear that Mr Finch is destined to continue to remain at the Old Rectory until the State decides he is so frail that Social Services must take him into their care. In the two years since we wrote about Mr Finch in the first edition of this book, nothing has changed.

Whilst the old man continues to exercise his right to live in the house left to him for his lifetime, the charity will have to wait for its legacy – a legacy that is diminishing as the years go by. As for the long-dead Mary Finch, she could not possibly have anticipated that, 20 years or so after her death, her chosen charity would still be waiting.

What should the Executors have done?

The Inheritance (Provision for Family and Dependants) Act 1975 allows an application for the evaluation of terms of a Will in certain circumstances. This would appear to have been a very suitable case where a negotiated settlement could have benefited both parties many years ago. Within our laws there are opportunities to make the most of any Estate for the benefit of all who genuinely have a claim. An efficient and effective Executor will ensure that the 'best deal' is legally secured for all parties concerned. In this instance the use of this procedure might have been a more humane one, in every sense.

One way could have been for the Executors to approach the charity and talk the issues through with them and their legal advisers. It is probable that they would be open-minded and helpful. They might have been able to offer a solution to ensure Mr Finch's future well-being and at the same time maximize the financial resource they had hoped to acquire, sooner rather than later. All charities have legal advisers at their disposal and it is possible that they would have borne any legal costs involved in an 'evaluation'.

If a solution could have been proposed then Mr Finch would have had to be involved at an early stage, and to have agreed to the broad principles. Who knows, he might have welcomed any ideas offered to make life easier, so long as he could maintain his basic lifestyle, where a very short walk to the Swan and his only real communication with the world existed. A comfortable, small retirement bungalow for him, perhaps rented on his behalf for his lifetime from a Trust Fund set up from the proceeds of the sale of the Old Rectory? There were some very close by. From the same fund the charity could have taken a modest annual income to help their work, with the residue going to them after Mr Finch's eventual death.

This is but one of many possibilities that could have been explored if the Executors had acted more responsibly, and efficiently, when Mrs Finch died.

CASE HISTORY 4
'Granny's Legacy'

When Mrs Lacey began to experience difficulty looking after herself and her large home, it was agreed that she should sell her property and move in with her middle-aged son, George, and his second wife.

George had a ground-floor 'granny flat' built for his mother at the rear of his house where she could have a few familiar pieces of furniture and effects about her while living semi-independently from him and his family.

It was a happy arrangement for some years. George's only child, Lynda, had never liked her stepmother, Jean, and had bitterly resented it when she and her father married two years after the death of her own mother.

Lynda was Mrs Lacey's only grandchild, and she loved her grandmother dearly, so when the old lady moved in the two spent many a happy hour together, to Jean's great relief, since it got Lynda out of her way for some of the time. The arrangement suited George, too. Most adolescent girls can be difficult at times, but he was for ever trying to keep the peace between his wife and daughter who were constantly at each other's throats.

Just after Lynda's 20th birthday Mrs Lacey had a stroke and died shortly afterwards. Lynda was heartbroken.

> 'When Granny died I just couldn't believe it; she was so hale and hearty and full of fun. Why, only hours before the stroke we had been having a coffee in the flat, giggling together over some nonsense or other. Honestly, it sounds awful to say this, but it was even worse than when I lost my mother. I was only a little girl when that happened and that was bad enough, but *this...*
>
> I had got to know Granny all over again when she moved in with us, and she wasn't just a Granny. She was a real friend with whom I could share my innermost secrets – things I wouldn't dream of telling to anyone else, least of all dear Jean, my 'so-called' stepmother.
>
> The moment the funeral was over they couldn't wait

to clear the flat out. Granny had some rather nice pieces of furniture, so they took anything of value for themselves and had the rest auctioned off somewhere. It was disgusting to see the way they pawed through all her things, all her little treasures, coldly deciding what could bring in a bob or two and what was 'worthless'. I felt like leaving home immediately – Granny was the only reason I stayed there for so long – but the fact was I'd just been made redundant and simply didn't have enough money coming in to finance setting myself up somewhere else, so I just had to sit there and stick it.

However, after I'd calmed down a bit, it did occur to me that Granny had been quite wealthy. 'You'll be all right when I pass on,' she used to say, 'I've got a penny or two tucked away for a rainy day.' I used to hate it when she said things like that, but from time to time the subject did crop up and now I wondered whether she might have left me a few pounds. If so, it might help towards me getting somewhere of my own to live, or at, least pay the rent for a little while.

She had a beautiful oil painting which she said had been valued at £6,500 some years ago and some lovely jewellery, notably a pearl necklace with an unusual diamond clasp and a sapphire and diamond ring, her engagement ring. All these things, she said, she wanted me to have when she died, not that I would ever dream of selling them, but the £5,000 (also promised) would have been extremely useful, at that time or any other.

There had been no mention of a Will, and I knew Granny had made one, because she told me so, but when I nervously asked Daddy about it he just said no Will had been found, and that as her heir, everything she had was his. I told him point-blank that Granny had wanted the oil painting and some jewellery to go to me, and he just said that he was very sorry but he had found no jewellery among Granny's possessions, and that the oil painting was his property now.

Jean had to put her spoke in, of course. 'I'm afraid you won't get your hands on that until your Father dies,' she smirked. '*If* he decides to leave it to you, that is.' I could have hit her right across her silly face. To make matters worse, I knew Daddy was lying to me because I'd actually seen Jean wearing the necklace, flaunting herself and knowing I couldn't do a thing about it. Daddy obviously felt really uncomfortable but was ruled by her, I'm afraid. The whole thing made me feel sick.

Eventually I got a job and moved into a girlfriend's flat, sharing the rent. I used to visit, for Daddy's sake, but tried to do it when Jean was out of the way. They had been living it up since Granny died, taking expensive holidays abroad, and so on, and often used to ask me to house-sit while they were away and look after the dogs. I was more than happy to be there provided the house was empty and they used to pay me a small sum for doing it, which was useful.

Whenever I was there I always used to think about Granny, remembering the happy times we had spent together, and one Sunday morning I took it into my head to have a nose through the attic. I remembered that when they had been clearing Granny's flat they had stored a number of supposedly worthless articles in the attic, and I just wanted to see them again, to remember.

To my great joy I actually unearthed Granny's old jewellery box, and thought for one glorious moment that I'd found the missing jewellery, but of course it was empty; Jean had got there first. I thought about asking Daddy if I could have the box; it was obviously of no use to him or he wouldn't have tucked it away in the attic, but it held great sentimental value for me.

The box had come from one of my late grandfather's business trips to the Far East. It was rather unusual, with all sorts of funny little secret compartments. If you twisted and turned certain bits of the carving you could open them up. I used to love playing with that box when I was little and tried to remember how I used to open it up fully. To my surprise, the bottom compartment clicked open and there inside was a piece of folded paper.

It was Granny's Will, dated some five years before, all

properly signed and witnessed and naming my father and her old family solicitor as executors! Most of her property, amounting to thousands of pounds forthcoming from the sale of her old house, had been left to Daddy, but she did specifically leave the oil painting and all her jewellery, carefully described, to me, plus the sum of £5,000.

I couldn't wait for them to return from their holiday, and when they did I jubilantly waved the Will under their noses. Daddy didn't know what to say, but Jean didn't turn a hair. She just calmly stated that I had found the Will too late and it therefore wasn't valid. She then proceeded to tell me I had betrayed their trust by snooping around among their possessions while they were away and ordered me to leave. Daddy said that as Granny's executor he should take possession of the Will, since her solicitor, old Mr Simms, had died a couple of years ago and his responsibilities as her executor had died with him. Like a fool, and in the emotion of the moment, I stupidly handed the Will over.

I could kick myself. In the cold light of day, I realised that if the Will really was so worthless, why did Daddy want it? To destroy it no doubt.

I haven't seen him or Jean since.

What should have been done when Mrs Lacey died?

It was of course quite wrong of George Lacey to assume that he was the only heir and was at liberty to take over his mother's property. If, as George claimed, no Will was found, the old lady should have been declared intestate and the Probate Court should have taken over and Letters of Administration obtained.

Even if a Will were found, it should clearly have gone to Probate because the value of her Estate amounted to more than £5,000.

According to Lynda, George Lacey was quick to claim all his mother's possessions since he held that 'as her heir, everything was his'. Even if we assume that George genuinely did not know that a Will existed, let alone that he had been named as an Executor, one could reasonably have expected him, as his mother's only son, to take it upon himself to search for a Will.

We do not know whether George Lacey did try to find a Will, but the deceased's solicitor should be an obvious line of enquiry for anyone serious about trying to find such a document. In this case, it is highly likely that if Mrs Lacey's solicitor was named as an executor, he drafted the Will. If George and his second wife really did 'paw through all her things' they must surely have come across documents of one kind or another which would reveal her solicitor's identity, although it is obvious from Lynda's narrative that George not only knew that Mr Simms was his mother's solicitor, but knew that he had died two years previously.

Since the Will was found in Mrs Lacey's old jewellery box, obviously Mr Simms did not have it in safekeeping. However, it is just possible that Mr Simms might have known the whereabouts of this Will, if approached. He might even have had an earlier (or later) Will in his possession.

We shall never know whether George Lacey did seriously attempt to find a Will, but in this case, as we have already pointed out, at the time of death Mrs Lacey was apparently intestate so Letters of Administration should have been sought.

What should have been done when the Will came to light?

Once again, family ill-feeling is a feature of this case history. There seems little doubt that without the influence of his second wife, George Lacey might well have come to some amicable arrangement with his daughter.

Obviously an injustice was done in this case, and the question that has to be asked is, can anything be done to resolve that injustice? Is it really 'too late', as George Lacey claimed when his daughter showed him the Will she had found?

Even in the case of a Will being found after Probate has been granted and a deceased's affairs 'settled', or if a later Will is subsequently unearthed, Probate can be applied for all over again on that later Will, and although it is a complex procedure, the Probate Registry staff will guide you through and prepare the papers to swear if you don't have a solicitor. There are cases, rarely, where this has been done successfully a decade or more after a Testator's death.

George Lacey, as one of the named Executors, should have administered the Estate and taken out Letters of Administration but he was clearly unwilling to do this, possibly because he realised that he had nothing to gain and everything to lose by so doing, so he preferred to attempt to sweep the matter under the carpet.

As Lynda said, all she really wanted were the necklace and the painting for purely sentimental reasons. She certainly would not want to sell them to raise money. Had she gambled on a court case, there were only the alleged words of the late Mrs Lacey that the necklace and painting were of any real value. Mrs Lacey might have lived with a fantasy – as can people at any age. She might simply have overestimated, or even underestimated. Without the evidence of a relatively recent and authentic professional insurance valuation document there is little point in pursuing the emotional claim.

Sadly, Lynda admitted defeat and decided to swallow hard and do her best to forget the whole affair.

There is recourse

Although she at present chooses not to do so, there is still nothing to stop Lynda taking action, although unfortunately she no longer has the Will in her possession in order to back up her case.

By interfering in the Estate (technically known as 'intermeddling') by collecting in assets, paying debts and distributing some items, George has effectively acted as an Executor. As such, Lynda, being a beneficiary under her grandmother's Will, can apply to the Probate Registry to have her father forced into taking out probate and administering the Estate as an Executor in the proper way. She could instruct a solicitor and the whole matter would probably be resolved and disposed of for a few hundred pounds' worth of fees. She might even have been able to make such an application herself with the correct forms and help from the Probate Registry. The fact that she does not have the Will may be a slight problem, but as the onus would then be put very much on George, he would probably feel that there was no future in hanging on to it.

3

Getting Yourself Organized

How will I cope with all the paperwork?

If you have read this far you have probably decided that you will fulfil the role of Executor. It is unlikely to be too onerous and should be made much easier for you if from the start you appreciate that everything will be smoother if you look upon the whole exercise as rather mundane administrative work.

Indeed, the 'Administration of a Will' is what you are about to undertake. Advice on handling complexities, at a variety of levels, is discussed later, but for now just think of yourself, and your co-Executors, as bookkeepers and stocktakers.

An unromantic role it may seem at the start, but remember that you have been asked as a responsible adult to look after the affairs of someone who was probably close to you, and whose survivors and beneficiaries now need your help. Much of the work is uninspiring, but a straightforward and systematic approach will make it all seem effortless and, probably, trouble free.

Don't trust your memory!

From *day one* do start to keep very detailed records of everything that you do, and certainly any expenses that you incur.

The obvious everyday comparison that springs to mind is the way that people in sales jobs are trained to record their activities, plan their calls to existing customers and potential ones alike, then keep records for future action and deadlines for that action to take place. Whether you have been involved actively in selling or not – and most of us have at some stage in our lives, perhaps without thinking of ourselves as a salesman or woman – you will probably have been exposed to the basic principles of good record-keeping and the importance of keeping them. Just think of the mess that a retailer or manufacturer would get into without stock control records for goods sold or parts to make an end product to sell.

You may be resorting to the old-fashioned quill pen (or Biro) rather than computerizing the exercise, but then the demands are not going to be as great as to require this unless you happen to have a home computer that you use for everything. Indeed, you will find you can do it all very easily by hand. The key to it running as smoothly as possible is simply to be very thorough and methodical.

Here are a few guidelines to help you work to a system. They are merely suggested for consideration and to help those readers who perhaps do not live daily with the routines of paperwork. Of course most of you will readily adapt and probably improve on them for your own purposes and method of working even if you have not been involved in such a task before. Apologies, therefore, for mentioning anything that might seem to be stating the obvious.

If you are one who prefers to do everything in writing then make sure that you have copies of all your outgoing mail as well as of that received. It is not beyond the realms of possibility (or the probability of human fallibility) for documents to get lost or mislaid. Sometimes it appears that there are conspiracies of the 'never received' nature, especially when you want something in a hurry. This seems to happen all the more if you are requesting money, or even a statement of moneys owed to you – in this case the Estate! Be prepared for the occasional frustration.

You will doubtless devise your own way of doing this, but a few suggestions might help:

- Obtain a large 'week-a-page' diary in which to record all correspondence details.
- Record all letters in and out and keep copies of them.
- Record all fax/e-mail communications.
- Record all relevant telephone conversations.

Unless you have a tape system which automatically records telephone conversations you must make precise notes which can be easily understood should you have to refer to them weeks, or even months, later.

Names of contacts must always be asked for and noted along with the date and time of the conversation. You should also make a note of any details and agreements made regarding who will do what and in what timescale. This could be very, very important when dealing with certain financial aspects of the probate where delays in carrying out your instructions could be expensive and cause a loss of value to the Estate.

The simple process of making accurate, clear and retrievable notes of all you do not only helps to pin down others on whom you are relying to act to help you but will allow you some recourse should there be any dispute or misunderstanding in the future.

Sometimes the bereaved are only too pleased to leave matters in an Executor's capable hands. In many cases, however, an Executor feels obliged to accept offers of help from well-meaning friends and family, rather than give offence. If you are in this position, there is an even stronger case for keeping appropriate records since, at worst, the whole issue could degenerate into an undignified farce where the left hand doesn't know what the right hand is doing, effort is wastefully duplicated or – even worse – tasks are not carried out at all because 'I thought *you* were doing that!'

Apart from anything else your records will help to remind you to chase where necessary. It can be almost guaranteed that it will be necessary in some cases.

The importance of all this detail cannot be over-emphasised and will become very apparent. More about this need will be covered in later chapters and case histories when you will be considering active dealings with banks, building societies, registrars of stocks and shares and so on.

What about the bookkeeping?

The correspondence diary suggested also needs the complement of basic bookkeeping. If matters are relatively simple then you may well devise your own system that easily merges the two on each page and copes with notes against the diary entries that clearly state and record any monetary transactions – which will be mostly outward in the early stages.

A separate 'cash book diary' might be worth keeping. An example of how this might be made to work for you is shown in Appendix 4 and is very straightforward.

If the elements are simple then you will have no problems so long as you are disciplined about it. You might even be thinking 'I can do this on the back of an old envelope'. *Don't*!

Executors have found some of the simple methods described to be useful. They worked them out for themselves and have found the discipline to be an easy one and very helpful in achieving the objective of 'getting it all over with'. A similar piece of documentation completed by a 'professional' would be charged to the Estate at a high cost – deducted before anything can be distributed to the beneficiary or beneficiaries.

By keeping accurate and precise records you won't be left feeling you are entirely on your own should some officious or inefficient clerk make life frustrating for you. All your paperwork, well administered and documented, will be to hand.

Setting up a separate bank account, an 'Executor's Account', is often helpful to keep track of the financial aspects of administering a Will. There may well be a need when a solvent bank account is frozen and where loans are needed to fund funeral and other expenses which will later be charged to the Estate. Often banks or building societies will pay the funeral expenses and Probate fees out of the deceased's accounts (subject to funds being available), if the bills are produced. Ask! This can save applying for a loan which will incur interest charges.

Always remember that if you know your facts and feel that you are being messed about you *must* go higher in the organization causing you problems. Never flinch from doing so if it becomes necessary to progress matters, even if you feel uncomfortable in doing so. You should readily find a manager who will be appalled that you are being treated with less than the respect that is due.

Executing a Will is a serious task and can be fraught with emotion. Anyone you are dealing with should recognise this. Fortunately, you'll find that most do and are very helpful. But, human nature being what it is … Be prepared and *good luck*!

4

Valuing the Estate

Establishing the Estate's value

Now you start on the bookkeeping part of your work. It really is a simple matter of listing and adding up everything the deceased had in sole name.

Even where the deceased may have been living in a state of abject poverty, an Executor should never assume that there could not possibly be assets worth more than £5,000. Indeed, we often read in our newspapers of cases where elderly eccentrics have died leaving large sums of money tucked under mattresses or under floorboards, or have been in possession of important and valuable artefacts.

It has been explained earlier that some assets in joint names will become the property of the survivor automatically on death and that Probate is not required to release that property. If the property is held as a *Joint Tenancy*, the survivor immediately assumes ownership. However, if the property is held as a *Tenancy in Common*, the deceased's share does not automatically become the survivor's. You must check the Title Deeds of the property to ascertain how the property was owned.

At this stage you need concern yourself only with those items that are in the sole name of the deceased.

There is, however, a point to be aware of here. An asset in joint ownership might well require the signatures of both parties to action, for example, a sale of that asset. The same will apply to the release of funds in an account where two signatures are required for any transaction to be valid.

At the end of the chapter, on pages 78–79, is a checklist which should prove a useful starting point for you. It is comprehensive, probably containing far more than you will have to consider. You can quickly draw a line through the irrelevant ones. Then, think if there might be some things owned but not covered by the categories on the list and add them in.

Make your own list of items which you must consider

When you come to be involved in such an exercise you will probably find that some or even many of the items are irrelevant. You might also think of items that you are aware of that should be considered. Knowing the deceased, or with knowledge that you have of their life, you should soon be able to build up a fairly clear picture of the assets.

You doubtless will face the occasional dilemma, more especially if there are items that either emotionally, or realistically, are perceived to be of value. Here again you must use your judgement and common sense.

Two situations that we have come across recently can illustrate this. One is that of a professional engineer, the other of a highly valued amateur artist. They merely illustrate genuine circumstances. In both instances, as the saying goes, 'you could write a book about it'. You will probably feel the same when you have successfully fulfilled your duties. Perhaps you won't, but you might...

The role of Executor will be an experience, in retrospect daunting to start with, but eventually all should work out well for all concerned.

The engineer, though largely desk-bound in the later stages of his career, always enjoyed using his hands and was very clever at so doing. He died at 86 leaving behind a mass of tools and equipment such as lathes and other power tools which he had been using regularly until only a few weeks before he died. There is no doubt that the interest/hobby kept him going for almost 25 years in his retirement. If his neighbours or family could not get a spare part for their ageing motor mower he would make one, such was his skill.

How could an Executor value the contents of his workshop? There were perhaps a few single items, or parts of his collection of tools, that might achieve £50 or £100 on a good day at an auction. A dealer was approached and offered £200 to clear the lot. That an insurance valuation for the collection would have been in the order of £5,000–6,000 to replace on a 'new for old' basis, to use insurance company jargon, was irrelevant in the circumstances.

The artist had in fact had a very successful career in the nursing profession. Painting in watercolour had been a passionate hobby throughout her life and most of her work had been given to friends and family. When widowed, she was too old to return to nursing to supplement her very modest pension and started to offer some of her work to local galleries. Her talent was such that a steady trickle of sales allowed her at least to run a car on the proceeds. As far as the Inland Revenue were concerned, her output and sales could never have been considered as a business. After the costs of buying paper, paints and brushes, plus framing the better results, she was probably working for less than 50 pence an hour! Even though her paintings sometimes sold for £80–120 apiece, and most were for far less, it is doubtful if she sold as many as 20 a year during her last few years. Much of her work was given to friends or donated to charities. The people who did buy them through local galleries or art shows did so for enjoyment rather than any thought of an investment opportunity.

When she died suddenly without having made a Will, her only daughter had the task of clearing up. The house was worth a fairly substantial sum and would be hers. That was about all apart from some of the usual mundane household effects of no intrinsic value. In all, and using a similar checklist to the one in this book, the overall value of her late mother's Estate was very closely bordering on an inheritance tax consideration.

There were some 750 finished watercolours, more than 100 of which were already framed. Should they be considered at possible selling prices? Should these be taken into the equation? And how should they actually be valued? The buying of art is such a personal thing that neither prices nor volumes of sales can be predicted easily. Sometimes the picture frame is worth more than the contents.

In both these examples, unlike carefully and deliberately purchased book, coin, silver, stamp or other recognised collections of value, which value will often have been insured by the collector, it can be difficult to define what is merely 'hobby junk' or a treasure trove. We all read of the house clearance merchants who have made their fortunes from buying up such 'junk'.

Here is the dilemma for the Executor. Like the Official Receiver trying to make the most of the assets of a failed business, you will want the best for the family or other beneficiaries. No one likes to pay the tax man more than necessary but you are by law bound to make, to the best of your ability and judgement, a fair assessment of whatever assets might have been left by the deceased.

This is why this book devotes time to this agonising issue. In the two examples above it is arguable that there was little asset value in either case. The cost of trying to establish one could well have been counterproductive. There might have been one or two of the engineer's tools of high worth to a collector, if that person could be found. The artist's work might suddenly be in demand after her death, probably unlikely, but who knows? Van Gogh reputedly never sold a picture in his lifetime! Some of those 750 paintings might be worth a great deal one day, but they had to be considered as valueless at the time.

As any hard-nosed negotiator would do, the Executor should 'write them down as valueless'. If any member of the family or a close friend expresses an interest, then let them be the ones to clear them away. They need not appear as an item on your checklist.

Disposal by way of gift

Within certain constraints, particularly where an Estate is probably, or even possibly, liable for inheritance tax consider-ations, it is usually acceptable to dispose of certain items by way of gift in any fit and proper way. It would be only right to consider the feelings of any surviving family as the Executor thinks compassionate or appropriate. It is always possible that someone could be deeply offended by being offered a particular item of the deceased's property. Equally, someone else might be offended by not being offered that item. Such is human nature.

Some subtle research among members of a bereaved family will usually establish personal preferences. With some diplomacy it should be possible to keep everyone happy, and even grateful!

A clause often written into Wills by those who advise professionally is 'To dispose by way of gift to such persons as they think fit my wearing apparel and other articles of household or personal use or ornament of trivial value or which they may for any reason consider impractical to sell'. This is 'catch all' legal phraseology, but one that is easily understood.

In more simple language this clause asks of the Executor:

- Is there a value in old clothes?
- Is the furniture and kitchen equipment *really* valuable?
- Are the tools in the garage worth much?
- Who would want a collection of pieces of paper daubed with paint by an amateur artist?
- The greenhouse in the garden might have cost £2,000 five years ago, but what about now?
- There are old invoices for a personal computer and bits and pieces – superior equipment could be bought for half that price today. What is the second-hand value?
- Is that ornament, a painting or a piece of ceramic or glass, perhaps, of trivial value or a masterpiece if put to auction?

This list could go on for ever. You should, though, quickly be able to establish any items that you might consider eligible. In most cases you will soon be able to work out in your own mind that the costs involved in trying to value the items that you are obliged to distribute or dispose of far outweigh the value of those items. If there is a masterpiece in there, which is not recognised until afterwards as having an intrinsic value, then that is the way of things. You acted to the best of your ability and judgement and that is what the law requires of an Executor.

Much money has been put into the hands of 'experts' to value Estates, often in the belief that there might be some hidden treasure left by the deceased. The odds are not favourable and it is usually the beneficiaries who lose out.

Family auctions (or auctions for interested people)

One very acceptable way to value, and distribute, items of moderate value not specifically listed in a Will is to ask members of the deceased's family or particularly close friends if they have a special interest in an item or collection of items. They could then make a 'cash bid' for them. The sum of the proceeds would then become an asset of the Estate and be dealt with in the usual way. Often this can achieve as much as the proceeds from a public auction after all expenses have been taken into consideration. It can certainly save a great deal of administrative workload and the process is known as 'ademption' (see Glossary at the end of the book).

Obviously, the beneficiaries of the residue should be consulted and be in agreement with such a method of disposal. Imagine a fairly large family where the sons and daughters all have their own homes and are perhaps quite comfortably placed. The Will might have been written so that the total value of the Estate is shared in equal proportions among the surviving offspring. Each offspring has their own home, furniture and the other items that go with their family life. Each might want some particular items from the Estate, which was, as often as not, always considered their 'family' home.

The house might be sold, but should all the contents go to auction or be otherwise disposed of (often *en masse*), simply leaving a cash sum to be distributed in however many ways? There is no need if the people involved hold a private auction. Generally, it is possible to get agreement among the parties concerned so that any minor anomalies in perceived values of particular items, or collections of items, can be sorted out so that each feels that they have a more or less equal share.

Another effective method of disposal sometimes used, especially where it might be appropriate to be seen to be absolutely fair and impartial, is to invite any interested parties to offer *sealed bids* for items.

If it seems that there are going to be serious squabbles breaking out, or worse a war, then the Executors have no choice other than to insist that all items are placed with an established auction house. Should this happen then those who are unable to agree privately are at absolute liberty to bid on the open market. This should only be used as a last resort.

In summary

It is quite within the Executor's powers to dispose of household items and the like to any person and in any manner that they consider appropriate. It is also important for an Executor, particularly one busy in their own life, to dispose of items in the most cost-effective and practical way. This could be as straightforward as giving a lawnmower, kitchen equipment or typewriter to a neighbour, bedding to a charity or a favoured pet to someone who would care for it.

The possible options before you could never all be spelled out here and, like many of the tasks you will be faced with, some could be bizarre. You have to use your imagination, resourcefulness and sensitivity to human nature.

An Executor is quite entitled to make decisions as he or she thinks fit. The judgement to be applied is your own in the majority of cases.

Remember, though, *you must not act in any way that could be construed as a deliberate attempt to act fraudulently*, be it against the interests of either the beneficiaries or the Inland Revenue.

Where an asset is to be sold, either under the terms of the Will or through a need to raise funds to meet debts owed by the Estate, the value that you work with is that of the net proceeds of the sale. For example, if a house is sold then the estate agent and solicitor involved will automatically deduct their fees before the proceeds are released. The same applies where other significant assets such as valuable furniture, jewellery, pictures or other 'collector's items' might be sold through an auction house, shares through a stockbroker, or anything through an intermediary who charges professional fees. You account for the net value after sale only. With cars and the like you just get the best price you can!

If the Testator had been involved with an association, club, group or society in any capacity where there was a responsibility for money then you might find that some was being held by the deceased. Usually such organizations will have two or three of

Estate value checklist

Some items you should consider	Estimated value	Date check
The deceased's home (if owned)		
Bank, building society accounts including Post Office Giro		
Beneficiary under someone else's will		
Bond and disposition in securities		
Cash in hand (including in hospital, nursing home, etc)		
DSS death grant		
Employer's death grant (gratuity)		
Employer's superannuation		
Estate abroad		
Gift vouchers		
Holiday pay outstanding		
Income from a trust		
Income tax repayment		
Incoming standing orders[1]		
Insurance policies (possible refund on cancellation)		
Invalidity pension		
Life insurance policies (incl. accidental death and travel insurance)		
Mobility allowance		
Motor car		
National savings certificates[2]		
Old age pension		
Overpayment of rent, council tax (including rebates)		
Pension from employer		

Some items you should consider	Estimated value	Date check
Premium bonds[3]		
Rents from property		
Repayment of TV licence stamps		
Salary outstanding		
Savings bonds (including index-linked 'Granny bonds')		
Shares, including those in cooperatives		
Stocks and shares (eg Treasury Stock, consolidated and public stock, etc)		
Total		

Notes

1. It might be that the deceased had, through a business arrangement or through a loan they had made privately to someone, repayments being made on a regular basis, perhaps through a standing order to their bank account. Here you would also consider any royalty payments through licensing agreements, authorship, etc.

2. A post office will provide you with a form DNS 904 (Death of a holder of National Savings Certificates) which you will need to obtain a valuation, with up-to-date interest accrued. The instructions on this are reasonably clear but if you have any doubts then your postmaster or one of the staff should be able to help.

3. These are 'face value' certificates and obviously no interest is payable on them. They may be left in the prize draws for 12 months after death and then cashed. If the Executor decides to reinvest them on behalf of beneficiaries then they may not be eligible for future draws for three months. Again, your postmaster will be able to advise on this

their 'Officers' as designated signatories on the bank account. It seldom happens, and is fundamentally wrong, but is not unknown, particularly within small organizations, that there is only one. Should you be an Executor in such circumstances you must contact the organization concerned and make arrangements for the transfer of their money appropriately. You must also clearly separate it from the Estate with which you are dealing. (See also Chapter 5.)

5

Liabilities

Establishing liabilities

Having found what assets the Estate might have, you must equally know what the deceased owed at their death. It is always possible that you might be more concerned about the liabilities from the start. It must be recognised that there are people, sometimes apparently comfortably well-off, who die leaving a grim financial state of affairs. Case History 5 at the end of this chapter is a good example of this.

If you know, or suspect, such a situation then you might have skipped Chapter 4. After reading this chapter then you can go back to it and see how best to rescue and realise any assets that there may be to help the beneficiaries.

In Chapter 3 it was recommended that you should set up a simple cash book and double-entry bookkeeping system. This chapter is about establishing the debit side. At the end is a *liabilities checklist* which you can adapt to your needs as suggested for the valuation checklist in Chapter 4. This is the ' other side' of your double-entry bookkeeping. It is simply a matter of establishing what should be deducted from what you, hopefully, find on the plus side.

It is the duty of the Executors to settle any debts that the deceased has left, assuming there are funds available. The Inland Revenue, it goes without saying, have a prior claim to any money owed on an Estate. This is covered fully in later chapters.

Debts are categorized in the following three ways, in order of priority for settlement.

Secured debts

Where a bank or building society has lent money for house

purchase or any other purpose they would have security by way of the deeds or perhaps a life insurance policy to protect their loan. Usually these are paid off smoothly following the sale of a house. The financial institution takes their money and the residue of the proceeds of the sale become part of the value of the Estate for distribution at an appropriate time.

Privileged debts

Any medical or funeral expenses and other costs that might have been incurred as a result of the death are the first of these that will normally be settled. If there are no available, or readily accessible, funds for these then it is usually possible for the Executors, or Representative, to obtain a temporary loan for this purpose. The cost of this would be a charge to the Estate. As already mentioned, if the deceased held sufficient funds in a bank or building society account, these may be paid on production of the bill. Also in this category come unpaid wages for anyone employed by the deceased. If the deceased had been personally registered, VAT may also be a consideration if applicable.

If the deceased was insolvent or bankrupt then obviously nothing can be paid. Otherwise, you can clear these debts as soon as you have money to do so.

Hidden debts

The Executor must make stringent efforts to discover any 'hidden liabilities'. An example might be where a 'hidden asset', such as significant savings, perhaps unknown by the survivors until after death, had not been declared at the time the deceased applied for particular state care grants. The Benefits Agency and local authorities are increasingly observing Grants of Probate and cross-referencing to find frauds. They will demand payments back from the Executor even if the assets have already been distributed. If a statutory advertisement had been published and no claim was forthcoming within the period allowed (see page 86) and Probate is granted, the Executor is not personally liable and the beneficiaries will have to pay. Otherwise, the Agency can, and will, pursue the Executor.

Ordinary debts

These are the ones you can identify using the liabilities checklist at the end of this chapter, which you will be adapting for your own needs. In theory anyone who makes a claim on the Estate within six months of the death is entitled to equal treatment and therefore you need pay nothing outstanding until all have been assembled and considered alongside the rest of the accounting procedure that you are undertaking. In practice, if there are funds you can release then it is perfectly reasonable and proper to pay any small amounts owing to local traders sooner rather than later.

You will probably also want to hand over any small bequests that are not being taken into account for the purposes of valuing the Estate overall, providing they are not of significant intrinsic value, as soon as is reasonable – something less to be thought of later. Typical examples of this might be items of clothing, an old family Bible, some used power tools, cutlery or china (so long as not a major collection which had been valued and separately insured), 'trinket' jewellery, an old fireside chair and so on. You must make decisions on what must be declared and accounted for, and be confident that you are not breaking any laws concerning the administration of an Estate.

In the second case history at the end of this chapter, Case History 6, you will read that Pauline thought that debts died with the deceased. *This is most certainly not so!*

A creditor can force an Estate into insolvency in the hope of getting at least a part, if not all, of the debt to them repaid. There are many tragic stories of this happening and the deceased's survivors, perhaps potential beneficiaries, being left without a roof over their heads because the debts incurred by the deceased were very quickly called in.

Some creditors will take a fairly lenient line if the amounts owed to them are relatively modest. The power of the media today might, if used against them in cases of serious hardship, be unwelcome if they stood by their absolute legal rights. In recent years there have been many examples of this, though all for modest amounts.

A classic example that we found in the research for this book was of a recent widow, a sole Executor, finding an overdue credit card bill with much interest accrued amounting to nearly £3,000. She knew her late husband was drinking himself to death, as indeed he had, but had no idea that the cost of it all was funded by a Visa card in his sole name. There were no liquid funds to pay this, and had the credit card company insisted then they could quite legitimately have forced the sale of their modest home. Mercifully they did not in the circumstances, but compassionately – and only because the widow's name was not a joint signatory to the credit card – they waived the debt. The widow was lucky in this case. After six weeks of agony and turmoil, she and her son were able to continue to live in the 'family' home. It could have been a much sadder ending.

Bearing the above in mind, as an Executor you must not rely on such goodwill from a creditor. Never assume! If you are left to sort out an 'unexpected mess' then approach the creditor and explain the problem with which you are faced and discuss the predicament with them.

Where do you start?

Property – if believed to be owned
It is usually the case that the prime asset is property if the deceased's home was purchased rather than rented. This includes both freehold and leasehold property.

If it was owned then you must quickly establish whether or not there is a mortgage, or any other form of borrowing, and on what terms. Usually it will be easy to establish through a bank account if there were regular monthly payments for this purpose if the property was not owned outright. If you understand that it was owned outright then it is important that you find the deeds to establish this beyond any doubt. It is unusual, but not unknown, for there to be spurious claims from a third party claiming the return of a loan made years ago when that third party suddenly hears of a death.

If a building society, bank or similar organization is still owed money they will be holding the deeds against the debt outstanding on the property. After the mortgage has been cleared it is common practice for the building society, bank or a solicitor to hold the deeds in storage.

Where the property was owned outright, as a general rule it is reasonable to expect that if you can lay your hands on the deeds and they show clear legal title for the deceased then you can proceed without further consultation.

For leased property, even if on a very long term, you must establish what the commitments might be to ground rents and service charges, if it is possible to assign the lease, and any other conditions that may apply.

Property – rented

You must find a rental agreement or rent book to establish the terms of payment. This is very important as you might wish either to end the payments as soon as legally allowed, or quite possibly transfer the agreement to another name to protect the roof over the head of a close family member or members living in the same home as the recently deceased.

Quite probably anyone left in the home will be aware of at least some of the details and will be able to find the necessary documents.

However, under the stress of bereavement people do become confused and simply do not want to know about such matters. Sometimes they will resent the very thought of 'papers' being disturbed – at least until the funeral is over.

However bullying or brutal it might seem at the time, as an Executor (whether you are close family or an outsider), you must try to establish the circumstances as quickly and compassionately as reasonably possible. It is necessary to protect assets and ensure that no inheritances are squandered or lost.

Other debts or commitments

In most households there will be the usual round of outstanding bills to be paid. Check for direct debits and standing orders through the bank account as these will have to be stopped.

A bank account in a sole name will be frozen so nothing will be paid out. If it is in joint names some payments that might become irrelevant on death will continue to be made. Subscriptions to a club, society or professional body are the obvious ones to look for in a joint account, as are any premiums for insurance policies on the deceased's life being paid through a joint account. The quicker you cancel these commitments the better. This will involve tedious letter writing or phone calls but it is something you will want to do as soon as possible. Remember, it is easier to stop a payment than to recover an unnecessary overpayment!

Some of the more obvious ones are shown on the liabilities checklist. If you were familiar with the lifestyle of the deceased then you will probably be able to think readily of other commitments that they might have. Though it is seldom necessary, if you are concerned that there may be other creditors then it is the usual practice to publish a small advertisement in the *London Gazette*, the appropriate section of a local newspaper, or even a national one if you feel it warranted. If the deceased was in business, a journal of that trade might be used. It is, however, unlikely that you would need to go to these lengths but if you have *any doubts* you must do so.

If you sense that the circumstances demand this degree of complexity then you may already be consulting a solicitor who will be used to this process, but you can easily do it yourself. A brief look in the classified advertisement section of any newspaper will show examples. You will find that they ask for claims on an Estate either by creditors or beneficiaries. Always there is a timescale for any claims. Provided no claim is made, you are quite safe to deal with the Estate on known facts after the expiry of the advertised timescale for claims. If you had not taken this precaution there is a danger, remote though it may be, that someone unknown could appear in the future who is able to prove a justifiable claim for money owed by the deceased. If the Estate has already been distributed, the Executor or Personal Representative can be held liable for that debt.

Tax assessments

Once you have researched to the best of your knowledge all the financial affairs of the deceased and have a fair idea of any outstanding commitments then you will be in a position to draw up a statement.

Now you have to consider what tax liabilities there may be. There may be none or they may be significant, but there is nothing that is not usually straightforward if you follow the basic rules that are laid down. Unfortunately the jargon that tries to explain these rules, together with the bureaucracy which can be slow and sometimes confusing, often causes Executors concern and frustration. If you have followed the guidelines in this book, or created your own system, and have put together a well-organized 'set of books' clearly reflecting the deceased's financial affairs you will find that the responses from the authorities will be more positive – and probably speedier. The Inland Revenue all too often have to sort out 'jumbled heaps' of paperwork supplied to them. Their answer is usually to make an assessment based, one feels, on the most money they can get. Given a well prepared set of 'accounts' to deal with they are probably more inclined towards a speedier sign-off. If the paperwork in front of them is correctly filled in and where necessary supported by understandable – *and believable* – documentation then it will probably be processed without protracted correspondence.

Inheritance tax (IHT)

In the context of Wills and Probate, this is the tax which is most relevant and most widely discussed. It is, however, probably the simplest tax to understand and the basic principles are set out here.

In essence, IHT will be payable on an Estate whose value is over £231,000. Any Estate less than this amount bears no IHT and this figure is known as the nil-rate band and is usually increased each year in the Budget. The present rate, from April 1999, is 40 per cent of each £100,000, ie £40,000. If the Estate is worth £2,231,000, IHT will be 40 per cent of £2,000,000 ie £800,000.

In calculating the amount of the Estate which is likely to be charged for IHT, the value of the Estate on the Testator's death must be added to the value of any gifts made by the Testator, which were made in the seven years before the death. The tax calculated on gifts made in the seven years before the Testator's death is reduced on a sliding scale depending on when, during the seven years, the gift was made. This can lead to some quite complicated calculations but it is necessary to follow the scales set out by the Inland Revenue.

There are certain reliefs and exemptions which help to

reduce the amount of IHT payable. The most important are as follows:

Exemptions

- *Gift to a spouse.* Any asset given to one's spouse whether during one's lifetime or under a Will, is entirely free of IHT. As an example, the value of a trading business run by a sole trader or partner for more than two years, or a shareholding in an unquoted company held for more than two years, can be disregarded for IHT purposes. If, therefore, a husband gives his entire Estate to his wife under his Will there will be no IHT payable even if the value of the assets runs into millions.
- *Gifts to charities.* Any unconditional gift to a charity or a political party, as long as the party has at least two members elected to the House of Commons, will be exempt from IHT.

Reliefs

A 'relief' does not necessarily provide a total exemption from IHT but does help to reduce the IHT payable. These can be quite complicated and a brief outline of the major reliefs are given below.

- *Agricultural relief.* This helps to reduce the value of an Estate to the extent that it contains agricultural land. For example, if a person leaves an Estate worth £500,000 in total including a farm worth £300,000 then the value of the Estate for IHT purposes is reduced by the value of the farm. The amount of the Estate bearing IHT then becomes only £200,000 and so is within the nil-rate band. If the farm had been let to a tenant farmer, then the value of the Estate for IHT purposes is reduced by only half the value of the farm.

  There are also rules applying to the period of ownership before death so as to avoid people buying agricultural land shortly before death and so reducing the value of their Estate.
- *Business property relief.* As with agricultural relief, this reduces the value of an Estate by a particular percentage. It will be reduced by 100 per cent where the assets consist of a business or shareholdings in unquoted companies. Again, there are rules applying to the period of ownership before death. The

value of the Estate will be reduced by 50 per cent in a number of other cases.

If an Estate involves agricultural or business property of any value you will probably be using a solicitor, but many people do now run small businesses whether as sole traders or partners. These businesses will enjoy 100 per cent relief from IHT. Where no solicitor is involved there is a Capital Gains helpline available and you can find the phone number on the Probate application form.

Who pays IHT?

Where IHT is payable the Grant of Probate or Letters of Administration will not be issued until the IHT is paid to the Revenue. Essentially, it is the Executors who are responsible for the payment of IHT on the deceased's Estate. Often though they are faced with a 'Catch-22' situation: they have to pay IHT before they can get a Grant, but they cannot realise assets in the Estate until they have the Grant and it is those assets which will be used to pay the IHT. In practice, the Executors will borrow from a bank to pay the IHT and then repay that loan as soon as they have the Grant and can start to collect in the assets. If the Executors can borrow the tax due from the beneficiaries then there will be a saving of the loan fee and interest plus a speedier payment of the amount due.

It may be that the beneficiaries are in a financial position that allows them to fund the payment of taxes due on the Estate in advance of probate being granted. This is obviously preferable to the Executors having to arrange bank loans for this purpose. It is an important question that should always be asked.

Which part of the Estate does the IHT come from?

Once the Executors have the Grant and have started to collect the deceased's assets, they must address the question of which assets are to be used to repay the loan taken out to pay IHT.

The Will may state the position by directing that certain gifts be 'free of IHT' while all others will be subject to IHT. If a gift is made 'free of IHT' then the tax will have to come from another part of the Estate. Usually this will be the residue. If the Will does not make it clear then some quite complicated rules come into effect, but in most cases the tax will come from the residue of the Estate.

Are there insurances to cover IHT liability?

Where an IHT liability is envisaged it is possible to take out insurance cover for this. There are many options available in the life insurance market tailored to particular requirements. Typically, offspring who stand to inherit could take out a life policy on the parents, or any benefactor, which would pay some or all of the taxes due on their Estate. A typical example would be a family with some wealth where the offspring were earning well and could take a 'joint life second death policy' on the parents to pay for any IHT liability. It can be tax-advantageous in certain circumstances. To do so requires careful planning of the affairs of both Testator and beneficiary.

When should IHT be paid?

Generally IHT must be paid within six months after the end of the month in which the deceased died. If late payment is made, interest will be charged. The 1999 Budget brought in a requirement for the provision of information regarding certain lifetime gifts and also greatly increased the penalties for failing to deliver an IHT return within the prescribed period. If you are likely to be involved with IHT issues it is strongly recommended that you contact your local Inland Revenue office for details of the up-to-date literature to guide you.

The IHT on certain property may be paid by instalments over a ten-year period. This includes land, certain shares in unquoted companies or where they gave the deceased control of the company or a business. The forms submitted to the Capital Taxes Office, a change in requirement brought into effect in April 1999, will allow you to state that land or shares are involved and so they will know that you are applying to pay the IHT by instalments. It should be emphasised that until the Clearance Certificate has been obtained no payments should be made to beneficiaries.

Certificate of Discharge

When the Inland Revenue is satisfied that the IHT has been

properly paid in fill they will give to the Executors a Certificate of Discharge to that effect. The Certificate releases the Executors from any further liability for IHT. It is also possible to obtain a limited certificate discharging the Executors from all further liability for tax except for IHT due under the instalment option. Sufficient funds should be retained until the Certificate has been obtained. Recovery from beneficiaries of tax may be impossible.

Estate liabilities checklist

Possible bills outstanding	Estimated value	Date check
Electricity		
Gas		
Oil		
Rates (including water rates)		
Mortgage payments		
Rent overdue		
Council tax		
Income tax		
Bank overdraft		
Bank loan		
Credit card accounts		
Local traders' accounts		
Medical bills		
Car loan		
Telephone		
Vet bills		
Benefits Agency repayments		
Check other accounts not part of the Estate (see notes with Estate value checklist in Chapter 4)		
Total		

Note

Remember, if you have any grounds for suspecting there might be others you must place advertisements asking for claims as described in this chapter.

CASE HISTORY 5
'The One-Man Business'

Steve's father had been running his own small newsagent's shop for many years. Although he had been quite ill for some months, his death nevertheless came as a tremendous shock to Steve and his sister, who rushed up to the Midlands to offer comfort and support to their mother. Steve commented:

> 'I didn't know where to start. Mum had worked in the shop for years, but left all the finances to Dad. I love my Mum, but she is not what you would call an educated woman, and hadn't got a clue what went on in the business.'

Steve's first impulse was to close the shop while things were sorted out and later sell it. However, a family friend, a retired accountant, advised Steve to keep the business going if at all possible. If the shop closed suddenly, he reasoned, all the goodwill and custom built up by Steve's father over the years would be lost. With no goodwill, a newsagency business could overnight cease to be a saleable asset.

Accordingly, Steve found himself plunged into trying to run a newsagent's shop for the first time in his life, while dealing with not only his own personal grief but also that of his immediate family, and holding onto a full-time teaching career in the South. As if this were not enough, as the now senior male and best educated member of the family, Steve was expected to know what to do next.

No Will had yet come to light, but Steve's mother seemed confident as to her husband's wishes as regards funeral arrangements, so Steve visited a local undertaker who proved most helpful in advising him about the immediate steps of obtaining a death certificate and registering the death in order that the funeral could take place.

Still in shock, Steve and his sister searched the family home for any documentation that would help them begin to make sense of their father's financial affairs.

'We drew a complete blank at home, so started on Dad's office above the shop. It was like the *Marie Celeste*. Dad had been working there right up to the last minute; there were bits of paper all over the desk, in a jumbled heap – even a cold cup of coffee and cigarette ends in the ashtray. Sophie, my slightly older sister, and I felt like vultures picking over the carcass, and kept looking over our shoulders expecting Dad to come bowling in at any moment and ask us what the hell we thought we were up to.

Funerals are expensive, and we didn't even know where the money was coming from for that, so we decided that our first priorities would be finding out what money, if any, was available, and whether Dad had any outstanding bills to be paid, because we didn't want every Tom, Dick and Harry claiming my Mum owed them money she didn't have. There were some bills. There was a frighteningly large one from the main newspaper wholesaler. It was a complete nightmare. We went through Dad's filing cabinet and started putting bits of paper into piles on the floor. Every now and then we got all excited when we found insurance policies stating that there would be such-and-such a pay-out in the event of Dad's death. Then we'd turn up another piece of paper saying that five years ago Dad had redeemed the policy and taken a pay-out of a few thousand.'

This sad pattern was to repeat itself. Gradually it became evident from the plethora of bills, correspondence and bank statements that the business had been failing for a number of years, and Steve's father had been systematically cashing in insurance policies and obtaining loans in an attempt to obtain hard cash to bail out the business. Steve began to realise that his mother's future financial security was in jeopardy since his father had not even kept abreast of national insurance contributions.

However, one glimmer of hope appeared at the end of the tunnel:

'Although there was a mortgage on the house, at least

the old man had continued paying into a mortgage protection policy right up to the day he died, and the mortgage was in joint names. It turned out he had been 'robbing Peter to pay Paul' to keep that policy going. Thank God for that. We'd had visions of Mum being out on the street, but at least, it seemed, she would have a roof over her head. What she was going to live on was quite another worry.

She did have control over their joint bank account, which luckily Dad had left alone so that Mum wouldn't find out what a mess the business was in. There was around £1000 there but that wouldn't last for ever.'

The house, then, was safe. Not so the shop, complete with empty flat upstairs used as storage and office space. That appeared to be mortgaged up to the hilt and entirely in Steve's father's name. His mother, seemingly, had been a mere employee. Was she going to inherit nothing but a pile of her late husband's debts? Things were looking extremely black.

Peter, the retired accountant, was a tower of strength. As a trusted old friend, he threw himself into helping the family. He was insistent that there would be no fees. For Steve and the rest of the family this was of course a huge stroke of luck, since to engage the services of a professional to tackle the job would have been very expensive.

'I don't know how we would have managed without Peter, because he more or less took over. He had apparently once witnessed a will for Dad, so knew there was one somewhere. I felt awful about letting Peter take on so much work – and he refused to accept a penny from us – but we were beginning to get under each other's feet a bit, and I was losing track of who was supposed to be doing what.

Remember I was now back into my full-time teaching responsibilities and living nearly 200 miles away during term-time. It was a case of the left hand not knowing what the right hand was doing, and I felt I was being more of a hindrance than a help. My job is a pretty full, six days a week at my school. Sophie had her hands full with two young kids. It was just so marvellous that Peter had retired from full-time work and was so generously giving of his time to help the family in our predicament. He seemed devoted to the self-imposed task and having known mother for years particularly wanted to help her. I was grateful to agree to let him get on with it, with me in virtually daily contact on the phone to see how things were going and what he wanted me to do next.

Before Peter got going, I never even knew what such terms as probate, administration and so on meant. Talk about a steep learning curve – I could've done with a book on the subject!'

With the precision of a trained accountant, Peter plodded through all the paperwork and eventually produced a complete list of all the shop's assets and liabilities. Fortunately there was no money in his father's personal name, nor were there any personal debts outstanding.

Eventually, the Will that Peter was sure existed was found. It named the son and daughter, Steve and Sophie, as Executors. Was this also a demonstration of a belief he held that his wife was not up to managing such detail, the same belief that caused him never to involve her more fully in the business?

Until the Will was unearthed in an obscure 'safe place' where no one had thought to look, Peter had been helping, working on the basis of preparing for Letters of Administration. Much of the essential work had been done. Now, subject to a few more details, they had the appropriate information to apply for Probate.

It was possible to process this quite quickly and the business and all other assets passed into their mother's hands.

'Thank goodness Peter talked us out of closing the shop as soon as Dad died. As it was, we managed to keep it going, keeping all our old customers, so at least when it was sold it would be sold as a going concern rather than just an empty shop, one of many at a time when small shops were closing all over the country, in many cases due to the recent introduction of the iniquitous Uniform

Business Rate. The property market couldn't have been at a lower ebb than at the time Dad died.'

Steve's mother did eventually sell the business – for a surprisingly healthy sum. It had been, fundamentally, a sound small business. It seems that the father, like many small shopkeepers, had just not been very businesslike in the way he ran it.

'Mother was able to pay off the mortgage and other loans and still emerge with a few thousand pounds which, on the advice of the ever faithful Peter, was invested wisely to give herself a small income on which she could manage.'

Conclusion

By an extreme stroke of good fortune, Steve and his family received a great deal of help thanks to the generosity of an old friend. Had they sought professional help from the conventional sources, the costs would have eaten up the small profit made on the sale of the business and Steve's mother would have had a very different future to look forward to. The advice might not have been so compassionate or objective.

It is obvious that much time was wasted initially, because, as Steve put it, 'the left hand didn't know what the right hand was doing'. Clearly, should more than one executor be named, or if a single executor accepts help from others, clear lists should be drawn up of exactly who is doing what to avoid confusion and time-wasting, and sometimes costly duplication of effort.

It is a great pity that Steve's father did not seek help when he realised that the business was in trouble. Apparently Peter was at one time employed by Steve's father to look after the financial side of the business, which is how the two met and became friends. We can only surmise that, in an effort to cut costs, Steve's father decided to dispense with the services of a professional accountant and go it alone. As we have seen, this proved to be a false economy and by his actions Steve's father placed in jeopardy the futures of the very people he had been trying to protect.

This story also provides a graphic example of the importance of finding the Will, even if there is delay and frustration in doing so. It also shows the benefits of painstakingly searching for other documentation that the deceased might have left behind which, as and when found, was invaluable in the administration process. They certainly allowed the widow to sleep in her own bed with a degree of comfort and great relief after all the initial highly worrying uncertainties. These issues are all the more important where the deceased had been active in a small owned business.

CASE HISTORY 6
'Two in a Fortnight'

Introduction

This illustrates a simple case, which apart from a cruel twist is a typical example of what the Executor will experience in most instances. Here the deceased was a council tenant leaving possessions with a value of less than £5,000 to an only daughter, nominated as the sole Executor. There was no need for Probate.

The daughter, Pauline, recounts her story and it is included here as it talks you through the fairly straightforward, though sometimes faintly ridiculous, events that can be experienced.

Pauline's stepfather, Harry, had become ill quite suddenly. Within three weeks of a diagnosis of cancer, he died in hospital.

Meanwhile, her mother was admitted to the same hospital and died exactly two weeks after Harry. When he died, Pauline had the painful duty of visiting her mother in hospital to discuss the funeral arrangements.

> 'I couldn't believe I was sitting at my sick mother's bedside asking her what she wanted done with Harry's body. It seemed unbelievably cruel.'

As a single parent, Pauline was torn between her duty to her family, two teenage boys, and her obligation to carry out her mother's wishes. Her cousin, who lived near her parents' home, volunteered to obtain the death certificate and visit the registrar of Births, Deaths and Marriages so that Pauline could make the funeral arrangements.

> 'My mother couldn't even attend her own husband's

funeral, she was so ill, and on the very day – just as the undertakers were arranging the flowers on top of Harry's coffin – the hospital sent for me because my mother's condition had taken a turn for the worse. I practically ran to the hospital – there was a public transport strike in London at the time and you couldn't get a cab for love or money – just in time to see my mother being rushed to the intensive care unit.

The ensuing couple of weeks passed in a daze, with my mother deteriorating by the minute. When she died very quickly after Harry, I had to go through the whole ghastly rigmarole all over again – death certificate, Registrar, undertaker. The Registrar almost greeted me like an old friend. I tried to keep calm and just go through the motions, not thinking too much.

My conversation with the undertaker was almost farcical. There he sat, this young man in an old man's mourning clothes, trying to be terribly solemn. I couldn't bear discussing all the details all over again. 'I want exactly the same arrangements as for Harry,' I insisted. 'Same day of the week, same time, same music, same everything – I don't even want to talk about it.'

When the young man asked if I would like an estimate, I curled my lip. 'I hardly think the cost of funerals would have galloped in two weeks,' I sneered, hating myself. I don't know who was more embarrassed, me or him. He shuffled his feet, coughed apologetically and had the nerve – or was it just naiveté – to say that the second funeral would be slightly cheaper than the first. I heard myself snapping 'What's this then, a discount for quantity?' Heaven help me, the words just slipped out, I was so furious. The young man burbled something about being £4.50 cheaper, out of a total of more than £1,700, because I had requested that their ashes be mingled, so my mother would not require an urn. It was unreal, like something out of Monty Python.

I stumbled outside and am ashamed to admit I couldn't stop laughing, tears rolling down my cheeks – hysteria I suppose. I bet that meeting will go down in that young man's memory for ever. Maybe one day he'll write a book on how not to deal with the recently bereaved and make a fortune. I probably did him a huge favour.

Do you know, I didn't have a clue about probate, Executors and all that stuff. I just assumed that as my mother's closest relative it was my absolute responsibility to go to their council flat and sort out hers and Harry's effects.

I collected every scrap of paper I could find at the flat and sat at the kitchen table and pored through it. To my surprise, I found two very simple Wills, properly witnessed, leaving all to each other and then naming me as their Executor. The Wills also stated that on the death of the last survivor I should have everything – not that there was actually anything much to have apart from one or two items of sentimental value. In fact, I got quite tearful as I glanced around the flat. Seventy- five years of two lives encapsulated in these five tiny rooms, with their ordinary bits and pieces of inexpensive furniture, their M & S curtains and their exactly two-week-old copies of the *Radio Times* and *Daily Express*. Seventy-five years' worth of bits of paper – among them their birth, marriage and death certificates and their Wills – and it all fitted quite comfortably into a Safeways carrier bag.

I can remember exactly what was in that carrier bag and what I did with the contents:

Bank statement in joint names showing a balance of £450	Wrote to the bank asking them to close the account. On producing the wills, personal identification and death certificates I was given the £450.
Building society pass-book in joint names showing a balance of £200	Sent the building society the passbook and the outcome was exactly the same as with the bank.

(These sums represented their total financial assets, as far as I could make out.)

Two pension books	Returned to the address given on the back with a covering letter.
Correspondence from an insurance company relating to a small occupational pension regularly paid to Harry	Wrote explaining that Harry had died.
Gas and electricity payment books	Wrote asking for gas and electricity to be turned off and bills sent to me. Settled those bills when they arrived.
TV hire agreement	Wrote asking the company to cancel the agreement and collect the television set.
Council rent book	Returned the rent book with a letter explaining the situation and asking for two weeks to clear the flat prior to its being let to a new tenant.
Cheque books, miscellaneous old correspondence, photographs, birthday cards, even drawings done by me as a child that my mother had kept over the years	Mostly destroyed but some kept back for sentimental reasons. I was particularly distressed to find love letters written by Harry to my mother. It seemed awful to destroy them but it would have been even worse for me to keep them – they didn't belong to me and were intensely personal to my mother. If I had just thrown them away some curious person might have found and read them, so I quietly and sombrely burnt them in the grate and shed a tear for my mother's lost youth.

Before clearing the flat completely I had set a time aside so that members of the family could visit and take any items they might want to keep for themselves. I had thought that this would be the most democratic way of doing things since rumblings like, 'Your mother always said I was to have her gold pendant' and 'I bought them that cut glass bowl when they got married...' left me sick at heart and utterly contemptuous of the covetousness of, God help me, my family.

I wanted to just shut my eyes, let them take the lot and get out of my sight, while praying that I could hold my temper in check.

They were the family from hell. They scrambled over each other to get their hands on my mother's modest little possessions. Curtains were ripped from the windows, hooks and all, rugs were deftly rolled and mattresses manoeuvred into the rash of small vans that materialized in the street outside. It was like the first day at the sales, only everything was free. I was mildly surprised to find the wallpaper and floorboards still in place when they'd gone.

Not that my mother's nearest-but-not-dearest – her neighbours – were any better. What few items of monetary value I knew to be in the flat had mysteriously vanished before I got there. I can only conclude that someone with a key had made a cruel, petty little killing. I couldn't prove anything, of course, and didn't have the heart to try, but I knew very well that my mother had been in the habit, like so many people, of leaving spare keys with two 'trusted' neighbours, just in case she accidentally locked herself out, or wanted someone to keep an eye on the flat or water the plants when she went away for a weekend.

My mother had been the proud owner of a few modest items of gold jewellery – a charm bracelet, one or two rings, a pendant, some pairs of earrings – lovingly bought for her by Harry over nearly 40 years of marriage. None were of great value, just of sentiment. Even a pawnbroker wouldn't have been interested. All that remained were a few worthless beads and baubles, so the pendant-fancier would have to be unlucky. I was regarded with heavy suspicion when I broke this sad news to the aunt in question, and half expected her to demand that I be strip-searched before being allowed to leave the premises.

A fine bone china tea service, my mother's pride and joy, had been found missing at mother's funeral when I needed it to offer tea to the mourners, but mysteriously reappeared, packed neatly in a box, by the time I began clearing the flat. A neighbour with a guilty conscience perhaps.

My son and I cleared what was left. Clothes went to a local old people's home and out-and-out rubbish was put into the giant wheelie bins outside. As we drove away, we were just in time to catch a glimpse of one or two of my mother's ubiquitous neighbours rooting through the wheelie bins. We just shook our heads in horror – too shell-shocked to do anything about it – and got the hell out.

When I got home I wrote a further letter to my mother's local council offices suggesting that before reletting the flat they should change the locks.

About three weeks after the funerals, I received a letter from the council asking me for two weeks' rent for the period immediately after my mother's death. I telephoned and told an embarrassed council official that I was not their tenant and had no intention of paying any rent for a two-week period in which I had emptied and cleaned the flat for them. They should think themselves lucky I didn't send them a bill.

There had been no outstanding bills as far as I could ascertain, apart from gas and electricity bills, which I paid, but in any case I was informed by a friend that a deceased's debts died with them. Whether this is true or not I don't know and I didn't care at the time. The expensive funeral costs were covered, though I did have to dip in my own pocket a bit, which I really couldn't afford, but then she was my Mum. You could say that her death had cost me. I had done the responsible thing for her. I had probably paid more to the various authorities than was necessary – so people tell me now. I simply did what I felt was proper and honest, and as quickly as possible. If anyone else came begging later then it was quite simple. She left very little. That money, plus, had been spent on a very humble funeral. There was nothing else. Fortunately for me no one challenged. How could they, anyway?

I did ask the post office to forward any mail on to me, just in case any more debts came out of the woodwork, but none ever did. The council were the only people who came with demands for money after my mother's death and they certainly didn't try very hard after my outburst on the phone.

One bright, little spot on the horizon which helped to restore my faith in human nature was a telephone call I received from Macmillan Nurses. Seemingly while nursing Harry, my mother had applied for a grant from them, and that grant, worth £100, had finally come through. As my mother's heir I was apparently entitled to it. I explained that as I wasn't nursing someone with cancer, I couldn't possibly accept it, and suggested that the £100 be donated towards their very worthy work.'

Might the Executor have handled matters differently?

There are a number of lessons to be learned from Pauline's story. First and foremost, do try to retain a sense of humour. It would have been easy for Pauline to become embittered by her experiences, particularly her experience of human greed, but a sense of humour – of the ridiculous even – helped her to come through unscathed.

Having said that, Pauline herself admits that 'letting the family loose' on her mother's flat was not one of her better ideas. With hindsight, Pauline now realises that a better approach would have been to contact family members individually and privately decide which of her mother's effects she was prepared to give to them, although she does point out that time was short, since she had to clear the flat quickly and of course she could not lose sight of her responsibilities to her own children and her own job as the sole breadwinner.

She could not conceive of bringing the family together to discuss the matter, and the whole thing degenerating into a shouting match between the various members, as she put it, 'all over a few bits of second-hand furniture. Hardly Blenheim Palace, was it?'

Imagine, if you will, the family arguments that might ensue with the disposal of items of more value, though still within the threshold, as opposed to the very modest contents of a two-bedroomed council flat.

In an attempt to avoid bitter disputes within families, or at least soften their effect on heirs, it is the Executor's duty to advise the heir that if a Will states that all property is left entirely to a named person, it is a matter of pure discretion of that person, and no other, if he or she decides to make gifts of furniture and other effects to friends and family. Under the terms of the Will, those belongings become the undisputed property of the heir, to do with as they will, unless of course there should be attempts to contest the Will, which is another story entirely.

Since the value of the Estate was under £5,000, Pauline did not have to apply for a Grant of Probate, nor did she have a great deal of paperwork to sort out, since her mother and stepfather had the forethought to organise their affairs very tidily during their lives.

One very important point which came through, was the notion of anyone with a key being able to enter the home and help themselves to the deceased's possessions. It could have been far worse, so the Executor would be well advised to secure the home immediately if it is left unoccupied, changing the locks if necessary. Otherwise, when the Executor needs to estimate the value of the Estate, it could already have been eroded by uninvited guests.

When Harry was pronounced terminally ill, it might have been prudent, in retrospect, for Pauline to have tried tactfully to ascertain her mother's views on funeral arrangements if possible – though admittedly his deterioration in this case could be viewed as so rapid as to preclude an opportunity to do this. Nevertheless, if Pauline had managed to broach the subject when Harry became ill, it would have spared both her and her mother that painful discussion of the subject at a time when her mother so swiftly became critically ill.

Remember also the important point that was made in this chapter about debts being a charge against the Estate. Pauline was wrongly advised by her friend about the deceased's debts dying with them. Fortunately the local council did not press their rightful claim in this case but were entitled to should they have so decided.

6

Applying for Probate

Contacting the Probate Registry

In Chapter 2 we discussed briefly the role of the Probate Registry. Through the book, and with some case history examples, it is explained where certain circumstances make this unnecessary. More often than not, though, you can expect to find yourself having some contact with them.

The Registry's all-important small publication to help you is *Form PA2*. This is actually an information leaflet and not a 'form' as described at the base of the leaflet. The form for you to fill in, currently Form PA1 (3/95), is shown as a theoretically presented example at the end of this chapter.

We have mentioned earlier that plain English is, thankfully at last, being used more frequently in official and formal documents for the benefit of the general public who might neither want, nor actually need, to reduce the value of an Estate by incurring the expensive fees charged by professionals for advice which merely confirms what is readily and freely available to the lay Executor on request for no cost.

Rather than quote sections of the leaflet Form PA2 here, we recommend a phone call to your nearest Probate Registry which will not only result in a set of their various documents being sent to you in the next post but will almost certainly create an opportunity to meet with them to discuss your role in administering the Estate if you feel that you would like their help and advice.

Often this can save a great deal of time and administrative work, on both sides, if you think it appropriate. If you are feeling a bit unsure, having never done it before, then work with the time-honoured principle of 'if you don't ask, you don't get'. Why struggle if you can find someone on the *inside* to help? This applies to all the, doubtless, many people with whom you might have contact in the course of fulfilling your role as an Executor.

Example of the Probate application form

While this book generally avoids reproducing examples of forms for all the reasons explained, it does so on the following three pages to illustrate the *Probate application form* (Form PA1 (3/95)). For most Executors it will be one of the first to complete. Crown copyright is reproduced with the permission of the Controller of Her Majesty's Stationery Office.

Probate application form

Please read the booklet HOW TO OBTAIN PROBATE

To avoid delay please specify in box below dates on which you will not be available for interview

Are you available for interview at short notice **Yes** ☐

No ☐

USE CAPITAL LETTERS

At which Probate Registry or local office do you want to be interviewed?
(See pages 6–12 of the booklet)

SECTION 1

This column is for official use

SECTION 2   Details of the deceased

1	Surname	True name
2	Forenames	

3 Are any assets held in another name   Answer YES or NO ☐

If YES, what are the assets?

and in what name(s) are they held?

Alias

Address

4   Address of the deceased

F/O

5   Occupation of deceased at time of death. State RETIRED or OF NO OCCUPATION if applicable

D/C district & no

6   Date of death _____ Age _____

7   Date of birth

L.S.A.
D.B.F.

8   TICK the **legal** marital status of the deceased, and give dates where appropriate

Bachelor ☐
Spinster ☐
Widowed ☐
Married ☐ date _____
Divorced ☐ date _____
Legally separated ☐ date _____

FORM PA1 (3.95)

Specimen Probate Application Form. © Crown Copyright

SECTION 3   The Will

This column is for official use

1 Did the deceased leave a will?
PLEASE NOTE that a will may not necessarily be a formal document

Answer YES or NO [ ]

2 Is there anyone under 18 years old who receives a gift in the will

Answer YES or NO [ ]

Date of will/codicil

3 Are there any executors named in the will

Answer YES or NO [ ]

4 Give the name(s) of those executors who are not applying and reason A, B, C or D

A – died before the deceased

B – died after the deceased

C – does not wish to apply

D – does not wish to apply now but may later

Name(s)	Reason A,B,C,D

SECTION 4   Relatives of the deceased

NUMBER
If none cross through each box

1 Give the **number** of relatives, over 18 and under 18 year old in each category
If none cross through each box
PLEASE NOTE survived means they were alive when the deceased died

	over 18	over 18
Sons or daughters who survived the deceased		
Sons or daughters who did not survive the deceased		
Their children who survived the deceased		
Parents who survived the deceased		
Brothers or sisters who survived the deceased		
Brothers or sisters who did not survive the deceased		
Their children who survived the deceased		
Grandparents who survived the deceased		———

2 Was the deceased adopted?   Answer YES or NO [ ]

3 Has any relative of the deceased been adopted?   Answer YES or NO [ ]

If YES give their name(s) and relationship(s) to the deceased

Answer questions 4, 5 and 6 only if the deceased died before 4th April 1988 or left a will or codicil dated before that date.

4 Was the deceased illegitimate?   Answer YES or NO [ ]

5 Did the deceased leave any illegitimate sons or daughters   Answer YES or NO [ ]

6 Did the deceased have any illegitimate sons or daughters who died leaving children of their own?   Answer YES or NO [ ]

Specimen Probate Application Form (cont). © Crown Copyright

SECTION 5	Details of applicant	This column is for official use

PLEASE NOTE that the grant will normally be sent to the first applicant

Tick correct box

1 Title   Mr ☐   Mrs ☐   Miss ☐   I.T.W.C.

2 Forenames _____

3 Surname _____

4 Address _____

_____

_____ Postcode _____

5 Occupation / marital status _____

6 Tel. No.   at home _____ at work _____

7 Are you related to the deceased   Answer YES or NO ☐

8 *If YES* what is your relationship in law? _____

9 Name and address of any surviving husband or wife of the deceased, unless stated above

_____

_____

_____

If there are any other applicants give their details as shown above   Details of other applicants who wish to be named in the grant of administration and attend the interview

When you return this form you MUST also send:
- **The original death certificate**
- **The orginal will (if there is one)**
- **The account of the estate (IHT44 or IHT 205)**

Now please refer to the booklet for the address to which you should send your application

Specimen Probate Application Form (cont). © Crown Copyright

7

Property, Insurances, Investments and Pensions

Property

The encouragement by successive governments through tax allowances, together with people's aspirations, have resulted in us having a far higher percentage of home owners than our European neighbours – indeed, higher than most countries in the world. Home ownership, even with a mortgage or other form of loan, usually represents the major financial element in the valuation of an Estate. For this reason its worth is going to be high on the list of priorities for the Executor to establish.

If a freehold

Firstly, you must establish whether or not it is owned outright and, if not, who has lent money. Examination of a bank statement would readily indicate if there are monthly standing orders or direct debits being made and to whom. Contact should be made with them to establish the terms of the loan and what is outstanding. Look for any insurance policies that might cover the outstanding moneys which are payable on death to clear the loan.

If the property is owned outright it is probable that the solicitor who handled the purchase would be holding the deeds. You should obtain the formal certificate that should be with the deeds proving the absolute ownership, and once Probate has been granted and if the property is registered, the Executor must inform the Land Registry (they have many offices throughout the country and you can find the nearest appropriate one from a local telephone book) that the property is now temporarily in the ownership of the Executors as part of the Estate.

If the property is in joint ownership, it will generally pass to the survivor if it is held as a Joint Tenancy. If, however, it is a Tenancy in Common, the deceased's share will pass to whomever is nominated under the terms of the Will. The survivor will retain their share.

If a jointly owned property is not specifically mentioned, it will pass to the survivor, or survivors, outside the Will. If it is real estate, all that needs to be done is to produce the Death Certificate with a letter requesting the Land Registry to register the changes in ownership. Where the property is owned by tenants-in-common, the Executors must check whether IHT and mortgages are to be paid by the beneficiary, out of the residue of the Estate or by the proceeds of a life insurance policy.

In the instance of a property being jointly owned by an unmarried couple as 'joint tenants', the deceased's share of the value will be counted as part of their Estate for IHT purposes. Just because it does not pass under a Will does not exempt it from IHT in these circumstances.

Should you find circumstances where there are heavy debts, or simply not enough assets for distribution under the wishes of the Will, the property might have to be sold to meet these commitments.

In whatever situation, there are inevitably more forms to be completed. The Land Registry have a Form 56 Assent or Approbation which they will provide and also a helpful and simple document 'Explanatory Leaflet No. 15' which will guide you, as well as several others prepared to cover a variety of specific circumstances. As with other formal departments of the state, they will assist should you have questions. Anyone can now obtain from the Land Registry, for the payment of a modest fee, information on any of the millions of registered properties in the United Kingdom, without being the owner. In the event of you being unable to trace a title deed or mortgage certificate, the Registry will be able to provide a replacement, if it has ever been registered, given proof that you are an appointed Executor.

Application for Assent or Approbation by an Executor must now be registered within two months *or the transfer of title will not be effective.*

If a leasehold

If the Will, or Intestacy, provides for the transfer to a beneficiary, the deceased's representative must inform the ultimate leaseholder, the Landlord, that a transfer in 'Assent' is to be effected. This must be done in writing and signed by the Executor or Personal Representative. If the remaining length of the lease is fairly substantial then you can expect the assent to be dealt with as a mere formality, though in some leases there are clauses stating that fees can be charged in this circumstance and some landlords have been known to be greedy in the application. If you experience such, there is little that can be done if the lease documents are legally tight. Simply, the beneficiaries lose out as any such charges will be have to be paid from the Estate.

Whatever the term of the remaining lease, it is still owned by the Estate and will be transferred to the ultimate beneficiary. It is important that they have a copy of the assent, and grant of probate, to prove ownership. Should they wish to sell at any time, the failure to produce such evidence of legal transfer could jeopardize or lose the sale.

Transfer

Once you have proof of title, all loans having been repaid where they existed, then the assent form can be filled in and processed. As previously indicated, if the property was in joint ownership, it will pass to the survivor, or survivors, automatically and be registered at the Land Registry on production of a Certified Copy of the Death Certificate with a supporting letter and the Deeds if available. If the property is still subject to a mortgage, the Deeds will be with the lender. If there is no borrowing, the Deeds, if not held in a secure place in the property, might be held by a bank or, often, the solicitor who handled the purchase of it. The Land Registry will normally process the transfer of title to the surviving beneficiary on presentation of a certified copy of the death certificate together with sight of the deeds.

If you are acting on behalf of others, the assent form is essential. If you, as an Executor, are a beneficiary then you are actually writing the assent to yourself. In whatever circumstance, the Land Registry will advise on the proper procedures, and charge you their appropriate statutory fees, to ensure that the new legal title is registered. The importance of getting these formalities properly completed cannot be over-emphasised.

Insurance policies

It may be that the deceased carried one or more types of insurance payable on death and you will want to establish the existence and status of these at an early stage. If you cannot immediately find the actual policies, which you would hope to find in a 'safe place' along with other important documents such as a Will and birth certificate, you might be able to trace them through bank accounts where regular payments would be in evidence.

Today there is a very wide range of policies on offer that can provide a lump sum on the insured's death; too many options to list here. In the event of the death occurring while travelling it may be that some special policy was taken out for the trip on which you can claim. If travel tickets are booked through the use of certain credit cards there might have been some death cover offered automatically.

Where you find there are policies then you will first want to stop any regular payments to them by cancelling direct debits or similar. With the details of the policy number and a death certificate, you can approach the insurance company for payment. Some may respond with more forms to be filled in. Do remember to keep copies of everything you send them.

If the deceased was in regular employment at the time of their death the employer may well have been providing life insurance as part of the remuneration package. Sometimes benefit from this is technically due to the employer, though even if it is they will usually pass it on to a widow.

Obviously, in the event of an employee dying while in service, the employer is going to be aware and many nowadays are very sympathetic and helpful towards the nearest family. They are also often generous. As an Executor you should make yourself known to the company secretary or financial director at an early stage to establish what financial provision there might be in the circumstances. The age at death will be significant for pension rights also.

Dealing with stocks, shares or other investments

Here again you are looking for physical proof of ownership and the nature of the investment, number of shares, etc. It may be that these certificates are all organized together in that 'safe place' at home or are being held by the deceased's bank or that the deceased used a particular stockbroker.

When all are collected together, an initial attempt should be made to value them by looking at the closing prices published in the quality daily papers, if possible on the day of the holder's death. It might be found that some shareholdings are quoted only on the Alternative Investment Market (AIM), until recently known as the Unlisted Share Market (USM). The *Financial Times* publishes many, though not all, of these.

If you are not able to deal with this matter until some time later, as is often the case, then you should obtain a copy of the relevant *Stock Exchange Daily Official List*, where you can also find AIM listings. For a small sum you can get back copies from the *Financial Times*. Alternatively the deceased's bank or regular stockbroker, if one was used, will supply the information.

When all the shareholdings have been established you can start the valuation using the prices quoted on the day the deceased died. If the death was at a weekend then compare the Friday and Monday prices and use whichever is the more beneficial to the Estate.

You will find two prices for each stock; the higher is the one at which they are bought and the lower the selling price. The accepted valuation formula for IHT purposes is to take the lower and add 25 per cent of the difference between the buy and sell figures. A simple example would be:

Holding no	Description	Prices quoted (p)	+ 25% on sell price	Value £
1000	£1 British is Best plc	685–697	688	6880

Having made a list of all shares on this basis you should then write to the Registrar of each company which you should find on a dividend warrant. If this cannot be found then it is usually quicker to telephone the company's head office as some companies do change their registrars occasionally and even the Register of Registrars which you should find in a local library can be out of date.

In your letter explain that you are an Executor (or Joint Executor) and enclose a copy of the death certificate. Ask for confirmation that the holding that you have found is registered in the deceased's name and that there are no unclaimed dividends or interest payments held by the Registrars. It is worth asking for prompt action as you are anxious to finalize probate documentation. Chase if they don't respond quickly – some are notoriously slow. An accurate assessment is important for probate purposes.

On sale the proceeds, which will be net of brokers' fees, are accounted for as an asset of the Estate.

Pensions

These can vary considerably and in some cases even provide for a capital sum to be paid on death. If this is so it would be declared for IHT unless there is a clause that allows it 'to be paid at the discretion of the trustees'.

If the deceased had a regular income from a pension fund then it must be informed of the death. A surviving widow is usually entitled to half that pension for the rest of her life and there may be other benefits. A letter to the Trustees or the secretary of the pension fund must be written asking for formal confirmation of what the Estate might receive under the scheme as well as confirming the position regarding a surviving dependant if there is one.

Depending on the flexibility of the Trust Deed and of the Pension Fund Trustees, payment may be made other than to the surviving spouse. This could be advantageous for Income Tax or later IHT purposes.

8

Intestacy

In Chapter 2 a few of the many problems that can be faced with Intestacy were touched upon. To cover every possible aspect of it would be a subject for a separate volume and these cases often take a great deal of expensive legal expertise – and time – to resolve.

The importance of making a proper Will becomes ever more apparent when faced with Intestacy!

Intestacy rules

Dying Intestate – married with children
1. If the value of the Estate is less than £125,000 the surviving spouse will receive all of it.
2. If the Estate is greater than £125,000 then distribution is as follows:
   (a) The surviving spouse receives £125,000 (plus statutory interest until payment) together with all personal possessions, absolutely.
   (b) The remainder is divided as follows:
      (i) 50 per cent divided equally among any children (for minors it will be held in trust until they are 18); *and*
      (ii) life interest in the other 50 per cent to the surviving spouse. This means that the capital sum cannot be touched. On the death of the survivor the capital sum passes to the children (in trust until 18 if appropriate).

Dying Intestate – married with no children
1. Surviving spouse gets a maximum of £200,000 (plus

statutory interest until payment) and all personal possessions plus 50 per cent of the remainder of the Estate, absolutely.

2. The remaining 50 per cent goes to the parents of the deceased absolutely in equal shares or, if they have predeceased, is distributed in payments of equal shares as follows:

(a) to the brothers and sisters of the deceased (or their children if the parent has predeceased). If *there are none then*

(b) to the brothers' and sisters' children at 18. *If there are none then*

(c) to the surviving spouse, absolutely.

Dying Intestate – single with children

The whole Estate is divided equally among the children at 18 (or held in trust until then). Should any child predecease the parent their share shall be divided equally between any children of the deceased child.

If a child is adopted out of a family, and its natural parents die intestate, their offspring are not entitled to inherit from the natural parent's Estates. By being adopted out they lose all legal ties with that family, but are entitled to inherit from the family that adopted them.

In summary

The Rules clearly state the order of inheritance for distribution of an Estate as follows:

1. the spouse;
2. children (or their children if they predecease);
3. parents;
4. brothers and sisters of 'whole blood' (or their children who then divide a deceased parent's share between them);
5. brothers and sisters of 'half blood', defined as having one common parent with the deceased, or, if deceased, their offspring;
6. grandparents if surviving;
7. uncles and aunts of 'whole blood' or, if deceased, their issue;
8. uncles and aunts of 'half blood', or, if deceased, their issue;

9. where no qualifying relative can be found, the Estate becomes the property of the Crown.

Property

If there is a property owned by a husband and wife as joint tenants (see Glossary at the end of the book under 'Tenant') then it will automatically pass to the survivor. If, however, they own the property as tenants-in-common the share of the deceased will form part of his or her Estate and will pass under the Intestacy Rules as explained in this chapter.

Partial Intestacy

This arises where the beneficiary of a Residuary Estate predeceases the Testator and no alternative beneficiary has been named. That part, and only that part, of the Will becomes invalid and that part of the Residuary Estate is then distributed under the Rules of Intestacy in accordance with the terms outlined above.

By covering the possibility of such an eventuality in the drafting of a Will, this situation need never arise.

Have you any doubts?

Should you be concerned that by dying Intestate there might be claims on the deceased's Estate from any quarter and that you could face difficulties, rows or bitterness, then it is strongly recommended that you take legal advice. There are often claims, however spurious some might be, as a result of people remarrying and creating 'family units' comprised of half – or stepchildren who might feel they have a right to a part of an Estate.

Case History 7 at the end of this chapter tells of just such a problem even though in that instance there was a clear, valid will. Case History 8 is a further example of the problems sometimes encountered by children of second marriages.

CASE HISTORY 7
'The Divorcees and Tragedy'

Introduction
Like Case History 2 at the end of Chapter 1, here is an example of Executors finding themselves in an unenviable situation, where their skills in tact and diplomacy were much needed.

It goes without saying that the situation might have been avoided if the Wills had been better drafted and more thought applied at that stage. However, who can reasonably predict how people's attitudes and emotions might change over the years?

The Executors in these cases were left with a fraught task which they had to sort out to the best of their judgement and ability.

Read the story and the thoughts we offer at the end. Doubtless you will have your own views on how it might have been better handled. That is what Executors are for!

Jim had been divorced for 10 years when he met Stella, a divorcee with two teenage sons. After a brief courtship, Jim moved out of his rented flat to live with Stella and her sons in her small bungalow on the East Coast. Months later, they decided to get married, with absolute support from Stella's sons, as Rob, Stella's elder son commented:

> 'Jim was the best thing that ever happened to my Mum. He had a good job and was able to give us – all three of us – a decent standard of living for a change, after all those years of Mum scrimping and scraping to make ends meet. It was great to have a Dad again, too. My real Dad walked out on us when we were little and vanished without trace. Mum got fed up with trying to track him down, and existed on benefits until we got a bit older and she could go out to work and support us.
>
> Mum built a career and did very well. Once she was finally able to force a divorce she was able to buy our house from the council. She had taken out a mortgage which she had been repaying for some years, but when she and Jim got married she had the bungalow put in their joint names. Jim really threw himself into our

home. He built an extension – helped by me and my brother, Mark – completely redecorated and rewired, and fitted a new kitchen and bathroom. It was a different place, and what's more, for the first time in her life, Mum could ease up a bit, and started working part-time.'

There can be no doubt that Jim and Stella were very happy together. The only cloud on the horizon was Jim's only daughter, Beth, from his first marriage. Jim and his ex-wife, Marie, had parted fairly amicably. The family home had been given to Marie outright, and Jim had moved into rented accommodation.

Two years after their divorce, Marie remarried, so Jim stopped paying her maintenance, but he did continue paying maintenance for Beth, kept in regular contact and continued to pay her boarding-school fees. She left school at 18 and went straight into a junior job in a London PR company, sharing a flat with some friends. Jim was no longer supporting her though he was frequently very generous with cheques for birthdays and at Christmas.

When Jim announced his intention to live with Stella, Beth, then aged 20 years old, was outraged, and threatened to cut her father out of her life for ever if he went through with it. Jim tried to placate her, but she refused to meet Stella or her sons, so, only with the sadness of not having her support, he married Stella, always hoping that with the passage of time she would mellow. But Beth did not mellow.

Rob continued with the story:

'Beth refused to speak to Jim from that day on. If he tried phoning, she just hung up without a word, and if he wrote letters, instead of just ignoring them she went to great lengths to send them back with 'Return to Sender' scrawled across them. She didn't send back birthday cards, mind you, because they usually had a cheque inside, but she never, ever acknowledged them. Even Jim's ex thought Beth was behaving like a spoilt, jealous little bitch. She tried to get Beth to stay in touch with her father, but it was no go.'

Time passed, and Jim seemed to resign himself to the estrangement with his daughter. Then the awful accident happened.

On their way home from a meal out to celebrate their fourth wedding anniversary, their car was involved in a crash. They were killed outright.

Rob and his brother, Mark, were distraught. Aged 24 and 21 respectively, they had no idea what to do, so rang Jim's ex-wife, Marie, who had remained on distant though friendly terms. Marie and her husband were very helpful and supportive, even to the extent of helping Rob and Mark to make the funeral arrangements. At the funeral, Beth was conspicuous by her absence.

The two boys still lived in the house and on nervously and reluctantly searching through Jim's and their mother's papers, actually found their Wills.

They settled the odd outstanding bills from their own pockets, and, with a sigh of relief, also discovered that while there was still a small mortgage on the house there was an insurance policy payable to clear this in the event of the death of the policyholders. From bank statements and other documentation it was apparent that Jim and Stella had been comfortable, managing on their salaries and putting a little aside as savings. Rob and Mark stood to inherit a third share each of the combined assets. There was some credit in the current bank and deposit accounts, just over £2,000, now frozen.

Under the terms of their respective Wills, written on DIY stationery, Jim and Stella had stated that all their assets should be shared equally between their three children, Rob, Mark and Beth, on the second death. As sometimes is the case, they had never considered when writing them the possibility of both dying in the same instant. Each had appointed the other, together with Rob, as Joint Executors, but unfortunately had not appointed alternates (reserves). As a result of the tragedy and in the midst of shock and grief, Rob, with so little experience of life, found himself the sole Executor.

Privately, both Rob and Mark felt that Beth should not have been left anything at all:

> 'After all, she had cut her father off cruelly and if Jim
> hadn't married my mum there wouldn't be any house to

inherit. Now she might come waltzing in expecting us to move out of the home we were brought up in so that she can get her hands on the money.'

Unsure of the effect this could have on them, and not knowing where to start with such matters, Rob had a meeting with a local solicitor. She established that both 'boys' ideally wanted to stay in the house for as long as they could reasonably foresee. Rob's career had only just started. He was not earning much but felt he could afford the upkeep, though certainly not a mortgage at this stage. Mark was in his final year at a local university and had a positive attitude towards being able to earn his first salary in six months' time and therefore also being able to contribute. For him, particularly, to have to find a new home during the months leading to his finals was a terrifying and disruptive prospect. Apart from anything else he was determined to get a good degree as his personal tribute to his late mother.

The solicitor was confident that she could negotiate on their behalf. She assured them that, while they must face the prospect of selling to provide the third share of the value of the house for Beth unless a mortgage could be arranged to raise this money, she would try to negotiate with Beth. This would involve solicitors' fees, of course; not possible to determine at this stage. Rob, in his naiveté, signed a form to enable the solicitor to act on his behalf.

However, a few weeks later, a bombshell was dropped. Not content with a third share, Beth quickly found a solicitor to help her. She was trying to insist that she was entitled to her father's 'half-share' in the property and other assets. Rob and Mark could share the remaining half, which she saw as their mother's half.

Weeks grew into months, as the matter grew more and more contentious with a great deal of mud being thrown from both sides. Rob did his best to ensure that his younger brother knew little of this as his finals loomed ever closer. At least the delays meant that studies were not seriously disrupted, though the subterfuge was agonising. The letters flew between the two solicitors on behalf of their young clients. Rob looked on with increasing anxiety, envisaging their inheritance dwindling to next to nothing.

Eventually, with Mark's finals completed, they took Marie into their confidence and were talking of throwing in the towel, however unfair it all seemed. Then a miracle happened; Beth suddenly gave in instead and calmly accepted the third share willed to her.

It came as a complete surprise to Rob:

'I don't know for sure what happened, but I've got a feeling Marie had something to do with Beth's sudden change of heart, happening as it did within days of us unburdening ourselves to Marie.

Knowing how mercenary Beth was, you can bet your life money entered into the equation somewhere along the line. Me and Mark have talked it upside down and inside out since, and we wondered if maybe Marie had offered Beth money to back off. I always remember Jim saying that Marie had married a wealthy man; we did meet him just after Mum and Jim's accident, and he seemed very warm and pleasant. Whether he was nice enough to throw money at Beth, we'll never know. Maybe Marie just said she would cut Beth out of her will if she kept on... Who knows?

Mark and I were almost speechless, with the relief of it all. We still didn't like the idea of her having anything at all, but that was Jim and Mum's wish and my duty as Executor to carry out those wishes. We were just grateful for no more picking over the bones – it had been horrible, an unnecessary display of greed or spite, and had left a nasty taste in the mouth. The only ones to gain were the solicitors and, in the end, at the expense of the three beneficiaries.

We sold the house eventually. We knew the only way we could carry on living there would be to buy Beth off, which we couldn't afford, and quite honestly we didn't want to give her the satisfaction. Anyway, what were we? Early twenties? Time we thought about leaving home and finding separate places of our own anyway. Mark's career was starting well and could take him overseas. My company was talking of moving me. Horrid though the uncertainties and delays were, the timing rather helped us both, looking back on it.

Thanks to Mum and Jim, we were each able to start anew and find somewhere to live. Wouldn't want to stay in the house after all that. Too many memories. Yes, our solicitor's bill came to thousands of pounds. We tried to challenge it but got nowhere. It was paid out of our shares of the proceeds of the house sale and the small bank accounts.

After all it was me and Mark and Marie who sorted it in the end. In fairness, probably just Marie. If only I had known then what I know now about how these things can be smoothed, all three of us beneficiaries would have had a lot more.'

In hindsight

Bitterness and dissension between children in cases like this are, sadly, commonplace. Even though Jim and Stella had the good sense to make Wills stating their directions after death, they unwittingly left behind a great deal of bad feeling, notably in Jim's daughter, Beth.

It is a shame that Beth was unable to forgive her father for her parents' divorce, even though it appeared to have been an amicable one; this would appear to be at the nub of her subsequent hostile relationship with her father. Fortunately Jim and his first wife, Marie, had remained on civil terms after the divorce, which was a blessing in this case, since it was largely the influence of Marie, in some shape or form, that persuaded Beth to drop her attempt to contest the Wills.

Advice for Executors

It was a few years after this was all cleared up that Rob told the story, now a very confident and philosophical 30-year-old. He learnt a great deal from the bitter experience and, while he could not have acted any differently then, he now knows that the situation could have been resolved without him employing a solicitor.

He could have gone straight to Marie, on an emotive impulse, asking her advice. She and her second husband would probably have prevented the affair being so protracted. As we know, they were the ultimate intermediaries successfully achieving where lawyers were failing – expensively.

The essentials of this case were:

- Rob as a sole Executor had to act according to the terms of the two Wills.
- A challenge was made by one of the three beneficiaries. In this case it is most unlikely that any court would have upheld it despite Beth's solicitor's encouragement. (See Chapter 10 regarding contesting.)
- Rob and Mark need not have lost any part of their rightful inheritance to what proved to be unnecessary legal fees.

What might Executors do in a similar case?

- Look at all the options, particularly making contact with anyone close to the beneficiary who might be able to mediate.
- Find out about the strength of feeling and emotion that created the challenge to the terms of this Will.
- Establish what is reasonable and what compromises might be helpful, if any. This has to involve personal judgement, not emotion.
- Apply for a Variation to the Will.

Remember that no Executor is above the law. However, reason and common sense discussed face to face rather than through letters on intimidating formal notepaper can so often avoid expensive legal wrangles where there are usually no winners apart from the lawyers.

CASE HISTORY 8
'The Nursing Home Resident'

Geoffrey was in his late 60s when he met Sylvia at a ballroom dancing class. Sylvia lived in rented council accommodation with her unmarried son Bob, aged 42, and Geoffrey lived alone in a flat in town. They were both rather lonely, having lost their partners some years before, and got on famously from the start.

When they decided to get married, Sylvia's son, Bob, was delighted.

'Geoff really gave Mother something to live for. She didn't want to be too far away from me, so they decided to sell Geoff's flat and buy something nearby. They fell in love with a pretty little cottage along the lane, but couldn't quite afford it, and there was no chance of getting a mortgage at their age. So I offered to let them have the extra money on a kind of long-term loan basis. I was able to take on the rent of the council property and started my own adventure of looking after myself – probably not before time.

I surrendered an insurance policy to raise the £7,000 they needed. This represented one-fifth of the total – the cottage was on the market at £35,000, a real bargain actually – and we agreed that if ever the time came when they wanted to sell it, I would receive a fifth of the selling price, whatever it was.

It was all a bit academic, really, because as Mother's only offspring I would inherit her property one of these days. Geoff did have a married daughter, whom he hardly saw, but prior to meeting Mother he had planned to leave all his possessions to her, as his only close relative.

Quite properly, Geoff and Mother made new Wills leaving everything to each other, making me their sole Executor. When they both died, the Estate would be split between me and Geoff's daughter. This seemed only fair, as the bulk of the money for the cottage came from the sale of Geoff's flat, after all.

There was no mention in either Will of the £7,000 loan, which I didn't think anything of at the time – well, you don't exactly expect your own Mother to do anything underhand, do you? Anyway, there had always been trust and understanding. I suppose I thought that there was plenty of time to sort that out at some time in the future. I didn't really think about it as a possible issue when they told me they had been to make new Wills and that they had both named me as their Executor; it was all down to that mutual trust.

They lived happily in the cottage for a few years and I

was on hand to do the odd bit of gardening or DIY for them, which suited everyone. I had begun to notice that Geoff's health wasn't too good and that Mother was having to do more and more for him, but eventually he was diagnosed as having the early stages of multiple sclerosis.

Sadly, of course, there is no cure, and while he was by no means totally infirm yet, he certainly wasn't going to get any better. A few months went by with me practically living at the cottage – certainly calling in every single day to see what I could do for them.

Then early one Sunday morning when I called in as usual I knew immediately that something was dreadfully wrong. I found my mother dead in the armchair still dressed, looking for all the world as if she had nodded off over a book the night before – except that one side of her face was oddly discoloured. She had suffered a massive coronary. It was a tremendous shock.

Geoff was fast asleep upstairs, blissfully unaware of what had happened, and I had the agonising duty of telling him. He was utterly distraught, poor man, as was I. I stayed with him all day and night while we started to try to sort things out. Over the next few days I scarcely left his side apart from having to make the essential arrangements for Mother's funeral.

It was obvious that Geoff couldn't stay in the cottage by himself long-term and I tried to persuade him to at least let me get in touch with his daughter to let her know the situation and ask whether she could help in any way.

Geoff wouldn't hear of it. His daughter hadn't been near him for years. She had not even acknowledged his marriage to Mother and had ignored an invitation to their quiet wedding. As far as he was concerned, his daughter was just someone from his past. The wounds were deeply rooted. I suggested that these circum-stances might actually help create a reconciliation. No! He made me promise that I would not get in touch with her behind his back. He was absolutely adamant about it. I had developed great respect and admiration for him – what could I do but agree?

Geoff did recognise that his condition was deteriorating rapidly, but refused point-blank to be looked after by the state. 'I'm not ready for the workhouse yet,' he said grimly, 'and I'm not living on handouts – always paid my way and always will.' I tried to explain that it wasn't like that nowadays, but he wouldn't listen and just got himself in an agitated, tearful state.

After the funeral and when he'd settled down a bit, he let me take him to see a private nursing home a mile or two away, just to have a look. It was a pleasant place, not cheap, and residents had their own little self-contained flats with their own familiar possessions around them, but with nursing care laid on.

To my great relief he took to it at once and agreed that he would move in. He was terribly upset at the thought of selling the cottage in order to pay the nursing home fees – though we did manage to get some help through the state – but eventually agreed that selling was the only answer.

Geoff was all in favour of moving in as quickly as possible, which I helped him to do, asking me to make all the necessary arrangements for selling the cottage and disposing of bits and pieces of furniture he didn't want any more. He fully realised that his health would be increasingly declining, and said that when the house was sold he wanted the money paid into a separate joint bank account in both our names so that in future I could pay the nursing home fees out of it, and look after any other matters for him. He was fully aware that he would deteriorate and that there might be some days when he would not be able to cope.

I put the cottage on the market and it sold it surprisingly quickly for £55,000. Amazingly, considering his condition, Geoff hadn't forgotten about the money lent by me when they bought the cottage – though I practically had – and insisted on writing a cheque immediately for £12,000 – £11,000 representing one-fifth of the selling price and £1,000 to cover the cost of Mother's funeral, which I had paid for.

When Geoff was fully settled in the nursing home I asked him, on one of his better days, to sign papers I had obtained from the bank closing his account and transferring all the funds into a separate account in our joint names against future fees. We got the Matron to witness Geoff's signature. What a relief! By the time solicitors' and estate agents' fees came out of the money, we ended up with around £40,000 in the account; enough to keep old Geoff going for a good long time ahead.

I visited Geoff very often as if he might have been my real father. As the medics had anticipated, he deteriorated very rapidly. When rational he still positively forbade me to contact his daughter. He kept asking if I had kept my promise. Up to that point I had often wondered whether I was doing the right thing. After only a few months he was increasingly heavily drugged and sometimes he hardly recognised me when I went to see him. By now he needed constant nursing care, and the staff were wonderfully kind. He would break down in tears frequently and kept asking why Mother wasn't coming to see him, which really upset me; I used to end up in tears with him.

Mercifully, only a short while later Geoff died peacefully in his sleep. Now I could be released from my promise and had to inform his daughter. Poring through his papers, I eventually found an address, but no telephone number, so I wrote her a long letter explaining the whole sad story, telling her all about the Will and the arrangements for Geoff's care and explaining as gently as possible why I had not contacted her before. I concluded by asking her if she had any thoughts on how she would like the funeral conducted, since as Geoff's Executor it was up to me to make all the arrangements.

On reflection, perhaps I should have arranged to meet her, rather than reveal all in a letter, because her letter back was a real body blow. My mother, she asserted, had been nothing but a 'cheap gold digger' who had only married Geoff for his money, and I had aided and abetted her in squeezing all his money out of him. According to her, I had forced her father to sign a piece of paper giving all his money to me and she would not rest until she received the whole sum, plus the amount I had 'allegedly' lent them to buy the cottage. She couldn't see that I was entitled to any of the money, despite what I had told her about his Will, since it had been her father's money that had bought the cottage.

I tried ringing her several times at the number given on her headed note paper, if only to tell her about the funeral arrangements, but she just slammed the phone down on me, so I gave up; I'd had enough.

Soon I got a pretty hostile letter from her solicitor setting out the 'facts' as he saw them and it seemed very threatening. After a stiff drink, I rang him and arranged to meet him informally to put him right. It meant taking a day off work and driving halfway across the country but by this time it was all that I could think to do. Part of me was worried about my money and part of me was beginning to be outraged. Geoff's daughter's attitude, and that of her solicitor, had started to harden me. I know I'd always been rather placid and my Mother sometimes remarked that I was too much so for my own good. As I drove I realised that I was being bullied and inwardly started to rebel against it.

The solicitor started out pleasantly enough and it seemed that he might be helpful. He soon changed his tune and became rather aggressive, after I'd shown him copies of the Wills and Geoff's permission to open the joint account, together with receipts from the nursing home for Geoff's fees. I pointed out that half the money in the joint bank account effectively, and I believed legally, belonged to me. If I wanted to be awkward I could insist that Geoff's daughter was only entitled to a half share of Geoff's share of the joint bank account. A quarter, actually! However, I offered my acceptance that, perhaps, morally speaking, Geoff's daughter should be entitled to half of what was in the joint account and I would be in perfect agreement to this.

He had the nerve to say he didn't think it would be 'appropriate' for him to act for me since Geoff's daughter was his client. He suggested, politely, that I go home and instruct my own solicitor with whom he could negotiate. Our meeting ended with the usual pleasantries.

On the long journey home I was rather confused but my determination increased with every mile. I had learned enough from that meeting to make me confident that, in law, as an Executor and also as a beneficiary, my initial interpretation was right. That I possessed a letter from Geoff's daughter describing my Mother as a 'cheap gold digger' made me even more determined not to give away one penny more than had been prescribed in the Will that I was administering.

I talked it over with a few friends who encouraged me in my belief that I had no need for legal advice. The Will was quite clear. In due course, I did it all myself and the whole thing went through the Probate Registry satisfactorily. I duly distributed the remaining funds according to the instructions in the Will. There was not even an unpleasant letter from Geoff's daughter or from the solicitor I went to see.

The Will had been quite clear in the wish for her and me to share the proceeds, so she got nowhere. She had instructed a solicitor in an attempt to claw back half the £12,000 paid to me by Geoff, demanding proof that I had indeed loaned them money to buy the cottage. This claim had no validity on the grounds that whatever cheques Geoff had written while alive and for whatever purpose were his business.

I breathed a tremendous sigh of relief when it was over and have tried to forget all about it. I never did meet the woman who caused me so much anxiety and rather a lot of unnecessary expense. I hope I never do.'

A just and proper outcome

The challenge that Bob faced as an Executor should never have happened. Unfortunately, there are times when the less attractive aspects of human nature and greed come to the fore, an attempt to grab. In this instance there was no chance of getting any 'free money', but it did not stop the daughter trying.

As Executors, we often have to write off events that happened in the past and over which we have had no control. However, in this particular case, the sole Executor knew that Geoff had a daughter from whom he had become estranged, and should have anticipated that she could create problems when Geoff died. Even if Bob had not known the contents of the Will, he would have been well advised to press Geoff harder at an earlier stage to allow him to get in touch with his daughter, if only to keep her abreast of events.

It was fortunate for Bob that Geoff repaid the loan before he died. There should have been, but never was, a written record of the arrangements made when Sylvia and Geoff bought the cottage, and if they had both died before the loan was repaid, there is little doubt that Bob would never have been reimbursed. Geoff's daughter would probably have seen to that. Being the closest relative as well as being the sole Executor, Bob should have had the forethought to suggest that some reference to the loan be made in the Wills, however embarrassing he might have found it at the time. If he had done this, he would at least have spared himself the indignity of some of Geoff's daughter's wilder accusations and the hostility that accompanied them.

Bob is a decent 'average' man. He gets on with life as a good citizen without being driven by great ambition. He was hardened by the experience. Sensing that he was being bullied he used his time and his brains to establish the simple basic issues. He could have been panicked into rushing to find a solicitor – he did not know any – the moment that Geoff's daughter put pressure on him through her legal adviser. He was also fortunate in having some friends and workmates to help and reassure him that the issues were clear and simple.

In this case it was clear, from the facts laid out in Bob's letter to Geoff's daughter, that it was unnecessary for her to pay anyone fees to fight this straightforward Will. Her solicitor must have realised that her demands were probably unrealistic but doubtless took fees to act on her instructions. After all, Bob had written direct to her and not through another solicitor so he was probably to be considered naive and maybe easily swayed. Sadly there are people who take on a cause, offering only the slimmest possibility of success, for professional fees. Bob was not intimidated, fortunately, and saved himself a lot of money as a result.

Bob followed the formal procedures and paid the appropriate fees on applying for Probate. With the documentation that he could show, and by simply filling in the appropriate forms shown in this book, the Probate Registry had no hesitation in rubber stamping his management and allowing the Estate to be wound up. You will be taken through the appropriate procedures in this book and will see that they need hold no fears for the Executor.

In so many of the case histories you will read, a death in the family is followed by bitter disputes between relatives. This is a sad but true fact of life and only serves to emphasise the importance of the role of the Executor in anticipating and hopefully deflecting discernible problems ahead. Apart from his duty to try to avoid moneys from the Estate being squandered on complicated legal costs, he must bear in mind his obligations to the bereaved in sparing them as much further grief and frustration as possible.

9

Understanding the Legal Jargon

As mentioned in earlier chapters, quite a lot of the official forms with which you will have to deal are quite simple to follow these days. Most departments of state also provide you with well produced explanatory booklets to guide you. Where appropriate, this book tells you which of the leaflets, pamphlets and forms to ask for. In most cases you are almost certain to be offered them, but if not, then do ask. They are helpful and you will need them.

Unfortunately insurance companies, solicitors and even accountants are not as enlightened as civil servants are encouraged to be. You will doubtless come across the use of some antiquated language and the incredibly lengthy and complex sentences created by them. It can appear that this 'difficult' language is used deliberately to confuse, and that they hope no one will bother to read the myriad of words written in very small print which allow them to disclaim responsibility for just about anything. Sadly, it sometimes seems true.

Solicitors love to rely on the terminology of the past. That is the way most of our laws are drafted and only with expert knowledge of them do lawyers pass the demanding exams which eventually allow them to practise.

The important thing for the lay Executor is not to be overawed by their jargon. If you are at all unsure about fully understanding the meaning (and implications!) of a word or phrase then say so. You have a right to have them explained and by the same token they should explain themselves.

Acting as an Executor, even if you manage entirely without recourse to 'buying' bespoke legal advice, you may well have some brief dealings with a solicitor. More importantly, if you have a problem which you feel unable to resolve without advice and feel the need to resort to paying a professional, you must not allow yourself to be bamboozled by the terminology which one lawyer or accountant might use when talking to another. They should never do so to a client. Be insistent on clear, plain English, explanations.

The simple questions, 'OK, but what does that actually mean?' and 'How does that affect me as an Executor in the work I am doing?' should never cause offence. Questions like these should always be asked if you are in the slightest way unsure of their meanings, or if you have suspicions of any nature or their intent.

A list of definitions of words and phrases that you are more likely to come across and may not be familiar with is provided in the Glossary at the end of the book. It cannot be definitive but should be useful. If you need more, or intend to become a lay student of this subject, there is a very good paperback reference book published by the Oxford University Press entitled *A Dictionary of Law* that is good value. The reference sections of public libraries in the larger towns are also at your disposal, of course.

10

Altering a Will after Death

The possibilities

Generally, as an Executor you will be required to act in accordance with the strict terms of the Will. This involves carrying out the wishes of the Testator even if you may, personally, not entirely approve of them. In certain restricted circumstances it is, however, possible to 'amend' a Will after the death of the Testator.

This may be done for tax reasons or, more particularly, to benefit a person who is not adequately catered for under the original Will. The most important ways in which a Will might be challenged or varied are set out in this chapter.

While there are a number of options available to the Executors for them to use their discretion in the best interests of beneficiaries, and possibly others, care must be taken and the legality of any proposed action fully checked. Case History 10 shows an example of where failure to act properly became expensive for the Executor.

Inheritance (Provision for Family and Dependants) Act 1975

This important Act allows certain persons who are, or have recently been, emotionally close to the deceased or financially dependant upon them to apply to the court, usually the County Court, for financial provision to be made out of the deceased's Estate. Given that an application must be made to the court you will almost certainly be wise to instruct a solicitor. This chapter is written to help you decide if you really believe that the circumstances with which you are dealing make an appropriate case for such an action. Emotions might well be running high and injustices perceived. A considered and balanced view must be taken before any legal challenge is made. The cost of failure could be disastrous.

An application for financial provision must be made on the grounds that the deceased's Estate as disposed of in the Will (or by Intestacy) does not make reasonable provision for the applicant.

The following persons may make such an application:

- the surviving spouse of the deceased;
- the former spouse of the deceased who has not remarried;
- a person who has been living with the deceased for more than two years as a spouse and has contributed towards the welfare of the joint home;
- any person who was treated by (and can be proved to have been maintained by) the deceased as a child of the family, such as an adopted child or a stepchild;
- any person who was being maintained by the deceased immediately before the deceased's death.

Any application must be made within six months of the Grant of Probate.

Whether or not 'reasonable provision' has been made involves the application of some quite complicated standards which vary depending on whether it is the surviving spouse who is applying or some other person. Effectively, though, it will be a question of whether or not the provision made under the Will is 'reasonable' for the applicant.

The court must look at guidelines such as the financial resources and the practical needs of the applicant as well as the size (value) of the Estate. Further specific guidelines are applied in the case of a surviving spouse.

The court can order that income payments are made, or a lump sum payment, or the transfer of a particular asset to the applicant. Also, orders can be made as to which part of the Estate will bear such payments and may vary the Estate so that if one beneficiary should lose out alternative provision can be made for them.

Disclaimer

This is quite simply what it says it is. A beneficiary may decide that he or she does not wish to inherit a particular asset or assets. There can be many reasons for this – emotional, inheriting an insupportable financial commitment, even a perceived insult. The beneficiary making the decision to disclaim informs the Executors, and that is that.

The beneficiary should be made aware though that once the asset has been accepted they cannot disclaim at a later date. However, having taken the decision to disclaim, which the Executor should have confirmed in writing and witnessed if a substantial bequest is being disclaimed, the beneficiary can exercise no control over the way in which the Executor ultimately distributes the asset unless a Variation was written into the disclaimer document. If the beneficiary does want control then he or she should consider a Variation as described below.

Variation

This is where the beneficiary requests the Executors to transfer an asset to another person (see above). The beneficiary can chose whom they want to benefit and can give up the asset even after accepting it initially. This is not possible with a disclaimer.

The Variation of a Will is usually done only when complex IHT considerations appear which might not initially have been fully appreciated. Those likely to experience the need for such considerations will probably already be involved with professional accountants and solicitors.

As a lay Executor, if you find yourself even dipping toes into water that seems as though it might boil then it is probably time to seek professional assistance before anyone gets scalded!

CASE HISTORY 9
'The Love Child'

It is a truism to say that even in the best regulated, most conventional of families, sometimes the most alarming skeletons come jangling out of cupboards on the death of a loved one, and the bereaved are left to pick up the pieces. This Case History describes just such a situation.

Only five years after The Rev. George Andrews retired, he died leaving everything to his wife, Molly. The couple had bought a small cottage on the South Coast to be near to their only daughter, Bridget, who now takes up the tale:

'For as long as we could all remember, Mummy had always seemed content to plod along in the background as Daddy's general factotum, the perfect vicar's wife. She worked tremendously hard supporting him in all that he did, of course. She really couldn't be faulted, and was much liked, but it was Daddy who commanded all the attention. He used to say he couldn't possibly have coped without her, but somehow no one really believed him; he was such a capable man and well respected in the whole community, not just among his parishioners.

When Daddy died, Mummy was only 57, young enough to make a new life for herself, and in spite of her quiet, slightly timorous manner, my husband, Peter, and I were fairly confident that she would be able to cope on her own, especially as we were near at hand if she needed us. Actually we did offer her a home with us but were faintly relieved when she turned us down. The children would probably have driven her mad within a week, anyway, cooped up in our little house!

I must admit it came as a bit of a surprise, a pleasant one, to witness just how well she did cope. We never thought she had it in her! She took up painting again, for a start; something she had abandoned long ago as she never seemed to have time for it when Daddy was alive. Her work wasn't at all bad and she had modest success in selling it through a local gallery. She also threw her energies into all sorts of community activities and was altogether a different person. Her life seemed very full, and we were delighted; we even used to make jokes about squeezing us into her busy schedule and ask if we ought to make appointments through her diary secretary!

Mummy soon had many visitors – mostly from the old days – and one elderly widower, Jack Collins, used to come and stay the odd weekend. We used to tease Mummy unmercifully about him, since it seemed obvious to us that he was courting her, but she just used to laugh and say that she was far too old for all that romantic nonsense.

Nevertheless, she gradually began to spend more and more time in his company, until he was practically living at the cottage, and Peter and I speculated whether they might marry. We really didn't know very much about Jack's background; Mummy was oddly reticent about it and merely told us that he was an old friend from her youth – before she and Daddy were married. We assumed he was an old flame from the past and that Mummy was too embarrassed to discuss it.

Peter and I exchanged knowing glances when Jack suggested taking Mummy to the Greek Islands to celebrate her 60th birthday. We were delighted, and convinced ourselves that this was just a prelude to marriage.

However, it was not to be. Sadly, they flew back early because Mummy had been taken ill. She made light of it at the time, saying it was just some mysterious 'tummy bug' she had picked up, but within four weeks of returning from the holiday, she was dead, having spent just two weeks in the local hospital in intensive care. The death certificate showed renal failure and cancer of the bowel.

We were in a state of complete shock and just drew into ourselves. Irrationally, I blamed Jack for taking Mummy away on that holiday. I know now that I was in a highly emotional state and said some very unkind things to Jack, which I later regretted. He had been hovering on the sidelines the whole time, and was, quite frankly, beginning to get on our nerves. We had enough to do without him fussing round, and while he was obviously deeply upset by Mummy's death, our sympathy and patience was beginning to wear a little thin.

He wanted desperately to help but I shut him out,

and, remembering Mummy's wish to be buried next to Daddy, Peter and I made the necessary funeral arrangements.

Jack continued to take what seemed to us to be an over-intrusive interest, which we resented. We began to make nasty little comments to each other to the effect that Jack had been sponging on Mummy, since he only appeared to have a tiny income and we knew that Mummy had been left fairly well provided for. Peter even made a small joke to the effect that Jack might have been hanging around hoping that he had been left something in Mummy's Will.

When Daddy died, Mummy told me that they had made Wills at the same time, leaving everything to me, as their only child. Peter and I found Mummy's Will while going through her effects and, as expected, I was named as sole heir and Executor.

Jack had turned up at the cottage unexpectedly just as we had found the Will, and I confess I took a certain cruel satisfaction in telling him about it. Unable to contain himself a moment longer and obviously in a highly agitated state, Jack blurted out some incredible story to the effect that the Will we had found had been superseded by a later Will, naming a John Joseph Masters as Executor. He knew about this Will because Mummy had asked him to be one of her witnesses.

We were practically rendered speechless by this revelation, as you can imagine. I had never heard of John Joseph Masters, and couldn't believe that Mummy had made another Will without informing me yet had taken her precious Jack into her confidence.

I coldly asked him for proof that she had indeed made another Will, and to my amazement he produced a photocopy of it, there and then, saying that the original was already with this John Joseph Masters.

Peter had remained completely silent during my exchange with Jack. Now he said slowly, 'Wasn't your mother's maiden name Molly Masters?' Jack had turned quite pale and sat down heavily on one of Mummy's armchairs. For a brief moment I wondered aloud whether John Joseph Masters might be some long lost relative. Mummy's maiden name was indeed Masters, and her father had been called Joseph.

'He is indeed a long-lost relative,' murmured Jack. 'Your half-brother, to be precise.' Now it was my turn to sit down, utterly unbelieving.

We sat up half the night while Jack poured out his fantastic story. Apparently at the age of 20 my mother had an affair with a married man, none other than Jack Collins, and became pregnant. In those days, illegitimacy was a terrible stigma, and as there was no question of Jack 'doing the decent thing' and marrying Mummy, her family sent her away to have the baby in a private nursing home. It must have broken Mummy's heart when the baby was taken away from her soon after birth and was adopted by a childless couple, a Mr and Mrs Palmer.

Two years later, Mummy and Daddy met and were soon engaged. Within a year they were married. Three years after that I was born. It seems scarcely possible that Mummy kept her secret from Daddy for all those years, but that is evidently exactly what she did.

She must have been horrified when a young man called John Joseph Palmer contacted her two years before Daddy died and asked if they might meet. We shall never know how she explained that meeting away, if indeed she did. Apparently the young man had enlisted the Palmers' help in finding his real parents, and had patiently tracked Mummy down through the nursing home. Once he had established that she was indeed his natural mother, he changed his name to Masters, by deed poll.

I can't begin to understand Mummy's feelings on rediscovering her son, after all those years, but I felt jealous and resentful that I had to hear about it from a comparative stranger. Mummy apparently told John Joseph the identity of his true father and he was eventually able to find Jack Collins also. In so doing, of course, John Joseph was able to reveal Mummy's whereabouts to Jack, who, by now widowed, apparently lost no time in contacting Mummy.

As the tale unfolded my initial shock gave way to great anger and bitterness. I mulled over the past obsessively, making myself quite ill and putting a tremendous strain on my own marriage. How could Mummy have kept her secret from my darling father for all those years? She had always appeared to everyone as the perfect vicar's wife, pillar of the community. I suppose that she had been, really; it was unimaginable that she should deceive anyone. How could she have begun to build a relationship with her new-found son behind my back? No wonder Mummy seemed to take on a new lease of life after Daddy died – perhaps she was actually relieved when it happened, who knows?

After she had recovered from the initial shock of finding both her son and his natural father, I just can't imagine what her emotions might have been. Whatever, she decided to make a new Will without mentioning it to me, and for that I shall never forgive her. Nor will I ever forgive her for naming her illegitimate offspring as her sole Executor rather than me. At the very least, I do think she might have taken me into her confidence.

At the time, I felt so bitter against both Jack and his long-lost son that I imagined Mummy had been manipulated into changing her Will. I resisted meeting my half-brother for a long time and refused to accept that he could possibly be an heir, due to his illegitimate status. It seemed so unfair that he had been out of her life for so many years, yet could just come along and claim half the inheritance that I felt was rightfully mine.

I was burning with the apparent injustice of it all, and convinced myself that this stranger could not possibly inherit and that the Will must surely be invalid. Determined to challenge John Masters through the courts if necessary, I ignored Peter's sensible advice – I would not listen to anyone by this time – and engaged a solicitor to fight on my behalf.

After looking into the case thoroughly, and having cost me quite a lot of money, my solicitor advised me not to pursue the matter but to accept that Mummy's second Will was perfectly valid. Even if Mummy had died intestate, illegitimate issue had a perfect right to claim on her estate under the Family Law Reform Act of 1987, and the fact that Mummy had made him both Executor *and* a beneficiary, with me, made her intention so clear-cut as to be above dispute.

Eventually, I had to concede that I had made a bit of a fool of myself and, with Peter supporting me, I agreed to meet John Masters, though with a very ill grace.

It was painful in the extreme to stand by while a stranger poked through Mummy's personal effects. He wanted some pieces of furniture, 'for sentimental reasons' as he put it, and when I accused him of merely picking out the more valuable pieces, no doubt to sell and make money on, he sharply reminded me that he was positively entitled to half Mummy's property, and was jolly well going to have it. If I wouldn't see reason and come to an amicable mutual agreement, preferring a battle through the courts over the division of her effects, then he would fight me for a fair settlement.

I burst into tears at this, and completely caved in, letting him take whatever he wanted. I took some of her more personal things also and the rest was auctioned. The proceeds from the auction and the sale of the cottage were divided equally between us.

This was all years ago. I haven't seen hide nor hair of Jack Collins or his long-lost son since, and quite frankly I want it to stay that way.'

In this case, as in so many others, a great deal of heartache could have been avoided if only the Testator had apprised the nearest and dearest of all the facts at the time of writing her second Will, if not before, however painful it might have been.

We have been told this story by a daughter who, while suffering from the shock and grief of her mother's death, had to cope with the discovery of an illegitimate half-brother. As if this were not enough, she had to face up to the painful truth that her mother had deceived her father over a number of years, and even when near death did not confide in her only daughter.

Since we cannot change the course of history, however, we can only consider what else could have been done to resolve the situation in a more satisfactory and less painful manner.

What could the Executor have done to help?

Upon taking on the responsibility it is the Executor's legal and moral duty not only to administer the Estate but also to ease the path for the bereaved. John Joseph Masters was clearly lacking in the latter.

By the time he made contact with his natural mother, Molly Andrews, her husband George had died and was beyond being hurt by her affair of long ago. Surely he, with his father Jack Collins, could have persuaded Molly to tell her daughter the facts. They were not to know, of course, that Molly was to die fairly soon after she made that second Will, but it seems heartless in the extreme that father and son did not even see fit to tell Bridget when her mother was taken seriously ill.

Still, as we have already stated, nothing can change the course of history and Bridget, for whatever reason, was kept in ignorance. It can scarcely have come as a surprise to John Masters that he was regarded with great hostility by Bridget, who had quite naturally assumed that she was Molly's only heir, and he appears to have handled the whole affair in an unfeeling, even aggressive, manner.

One must assume that a young man determined enough to track down both his parents over many years was aware of his rights of inheritance. At the very least he could have saved Bridget, his half-sister, unnecessary expense in engaging a solicitor – *if* he had wanted to – by approaching her in a more sympathetic manner and discussing the matter calmly with her.

We did not meet the young man, of course, and have only heard Bridget's side of the story. We can only guess at his feelings. What a cruel blow it must have been, to discover his mother after all those years, only to have her snatched away from him once again. It seems clear that he resented Bridget, just as she resented him, and was in no mood to be helpful towards a young woman who had, unlike himself, enjoyed the presence of a loving mother all her life. Whatever his motives, John Masters was clearly in dereliction of his duties as an Executor.

While one can quite imagine Molly Andrews' joy in finding her son, and her recognition of him by appointing him as her Executor, it is actually a great pity that he was appointed at all. Molly would have been wiser to appoint someone who would not allow emotion to cloud their judgement and would thus be able to carry out their duties in a fair, compassionate and impartial manner.

Indeed, anyone agreeing to be an Executor should perhaps think carefully about whether he or she is perhaps so close to the Testator as to be unable to carry out the required duties in the manner that the Testator would wish. If it is felt that to be totally objective and impartial is going to be too difficult a responsibility, then the appointed Executor must refuse to act.

CASE HISTORY 10
'St Mary's Legacy'

Despite having undergone extensive heart surgery five years earlier, at the age of 72, David Ames continued to be a keen and energetic communicant as well as serving as Churchwarden at his local church, St Mary's. For 30 years the church had been his life, but even more so since the death of his wife, Margaret, three years before.

The Rev James Burton, vicar of St Mary's, had been a lifelong friend, and he and David had grown even closer after Margaret's death. To David's dismay, when James decided to retire a new young female vicar was appointed.

Within three months of the new appointment it was painfully apparent that The Rev Jenny Hooper's youthful enthusiasm, even brashness, was not appreciated by older members of the congregation such as the Churchwarden David Ames. The two were constantly at loggerheads, culminating in David's resignation as Churchwarden following a particularly spectacular row at a meeting of the Parochial Church Council. David swore never to set foot in St Mary's again so long as the Rev Hooper was in office.

Three days after his resignation, David had a massive heart attack and died.

David's children, Melissa and Alistair, as Joint Executors, requested that the funeral service be conducted at St Mary's by the former vicar, the Rev Burton. Alistair now takes up the tale:

> 'To our horror, the Hooper woman flatly refused to allow the funeral service to take place unless she officiated herself. We knew that her and Dad had loathed each other – God knows Dad had bent our ears back about it on countless occasions – but we just couldn't believe a so-called Christian could be that vindictive. Anyway, in complete disgust, and rather than be bullied by the woman, we arranged for the service to take place in another local church.
>
> You can imagine, then, how I felt when I read Dad's Will, written some years ago when James Burton was still in office. He'd requested that 1 per cent of his Estate – about £3,000 – be left to St Mary's for the Restoration Fund.
>
> Mel and I were up in arms about it, especially as only a couple of weeks before he died, when my wife and I took him out to dinner for his birthday, he was practically frothing at the mouth about the new vicar and talking about changing his Will. I didn't make the connection at the time, as Dad had never actually told me anything about the contents of his Will, but I can certainly see it now. It was transparently obvious to me and Mel that, what with the suddenness of Dad's heart attack, he'd simply not had time to alter his Will as he'd intended.
>
> We determined that no way was Hooper going to get her hands on the money, so we discussed sending the £3,000 to one of Dad's favourite charities instead, one that Dad had supported all his life – also a 'Faith'-based one. We felt sure that given the circumstances, this Church would understand and endorse our decision.'

Three years after David's death, the Rev Hooper wrote to Alistair, requesting that a cheque be sent to the Parochial Church Council by return.

Alistair wrote a furious letter in reply, explaining the family's reasons for failing to send money to St Mary's. In no uncertain terms he stated that it would be hypocritical of the Church to accept a gift of £3,000 in the circumstances, and urged the Rev Hooper to agree to the money being paid instead to a charity of the family's choice.

The Rev Hooper refused, and over the ensuing months the correspondence between the two became increasingly acrimonious, with both sides raking over the ashes of previous grievances. Appeals by Alistair to higher authority within the Church were to no avail.

Backed by legal advice, the Rev Hooper continued to press for payment of the Bequest on behalf of the Parochial Church Council, plus interest at 7.5 per cent from the date that other beneficiaries to David's Will received their cheques in settlement, finally placing the matter in the hands of the PCC's solicitor.

Alistair continues:

> 'I never dreamed that woman would actually hide behind the PCC's solicitors, but that is exactly what she did, refusing all further contact with me. My sister, Mel, wasn't a lot of help, I have to say. She had been quite content to leave it to me to sort out Dad's Estate, but at the first whiff of legal complications I'm afraid she completely lost her nerve and urged me to hand over the money and have done with it.
>
> Of course, with Mel's full agreement, I'd already sent a cheque to the charity we'd decided on, taking a bit of a gamble, I suppose, that the Church would waive their right to the money. How wrong can you be? Anyway, I was blowed if I was going to spend even more money instructing a solicitor to fight it, so in the end Mel and I each contributed £1,500 out of our own inheritances and I sent the PCC's solicitors a cheque for the £3,000. I also enclosed a receipt for the identical sum that had been sent to charity and, in a last ditch stand for justice, urged them to try and make Hooper see it would be quite dishonest to accept the money. Much good that did me.

All I got for my pains was a letter from the solicitors warning me against making libellous statements about the Rev Hooper, disputing the sum I had sent and demanding further detail on Dad's assets at the time of his death. As if this were not enough, they enclosed their bill for nearly £300 which I was expected to pay. They even had the cheek to question my expenses, as Dad's Executor. I mean, how petty and insulting can you get? Anybody'd think I was trying to make a profit out of Dad's death. Quite frankly, the whole mess was beginning to make me ill, not to mention what it was doing to my relationship with my sister, Mel.

When I showed Mel this latest letter she was apoplectic. She said I was responsible for getting us into this mess and that I should be responsible for getting us out of it. It was a real blow, I can tell you. After all, at first she was happy enough for me to do all the donkey work, but as soon as the going got tough she was ready to throw in the towel; she even started joining the opposition in making noises about my Executor's expenses being a bit much and wanted to know how I'd managed to claim two-and-a-half thousand for them.

Father had written into his Will that the Executors, my sister and I, could charge reasonable expenses against his Estate to sort out his affairs after his death. He wanted us to gain maximum benefit from the inheritance that he would be leaving to his 'two offspring' and did not want 'those lawyers' taking half of it. Father was fit when he wrote his Will and seemingly had many more years ahead of him.

'That's a hell of a lot of phone calls,' she said bitterly. Honest to God, I never thought my own sister would turn on me in this way and we ended up having a blazing row.

Mel said my pigheadedness would end up losing what was left of my inheritance and she wasn't going to see her own money sacrificed on what she termed 'the altar of my arrogance and stupidity'. She then engaged a solicitor in order to get herself off the hook and thoroughly distanced herself from my actions. I haven't seen my sister Mel from that day to this.'

One year on from the Rev Hooper's original letter to Alistair requesting the St Mary's Legacy, Alistair had reached the end of his tether. In a letter to a higher Church authority, he agreed to pay the interest demanded in instalments over one year, but the PCC's solicitors were still not satisfied that the interest, nor indeed the amount already paid to the Church, had been correctly calculated.

The argument continues to escalate, as do the legal costs which Alistair will be expected to pay. At the time of going to press, more than four years after his father's death, Alistair Ames is now awaiting a summons to appear in court.

CONCLUSION

Was the Executor justified in attempting to change the Will?

Whilst the authors initially had every sympathy with Alistair in the above Case Study, and it could be argued that the Rev Hooper did not behave in a manner that was sensitive to the circumstances experienced by the family, the Executor had no right to ignore his father's express wishes as clearly set out in his Will. Further subtle questioning, and analysis of many documents, made it clear that he had acted improperly and impetuously; emotions took over.

Despite the acrimony known to exist between David Ames and the Rev Hooper, and notwithstanding the alleged conversation with his son in which David stated his intention to change his Will, the Executor was quite wrong to simply ignore the clear instructions in David's Will. In Alistair's own words, he took a gamble when he sent the bequest intended for St Mary's to his father's favourite charity and unfortunately for him the gamble did not pay off. Alistair has only himself to blame for his high-handed action.

The fact that it was not until three years after the death of David Ames that the Rev Hooper began to press for payment of the sum due to St Mary's Church suggests that Alistair Ames simply stuck his head in the sand and hoped the problem would go away. When challenged he prevaricated to such an extent and over such a lengthy period that the Rev Hooper, acting on behalf of the Parochial Church Council, sought legal advice and began demanding interest on the sum due, dating back to when other beneficiaries had received their legacies. The Rev Hooper was quite within her rights since the Executor was in breach of trust in preferring and paying other residuary legatees in priority to St Mary's Church.

It is a great pity that Alistair doggedly refused to instruct a solicitor. Any reputable solicitor would surely have advised him to pay up and save himself and his family a tremendous amount of heartache, not to mention further personal cost. His sister Mel was wise to engage a solicitor in order to distance herself from Alistair's actions, or she would have found herself, as co-Executor, being forced to account for herself in court alongside her brother.

In the event, intransigence on both sides meant the argument wore on to the point where the Rev Hooper, backed by the Parochial Church Council and all the might of the Church's Legal Department, took this Executor to court. We do not yet know the outcome of this action but the costs, Alistair's legal fees, interest rate charges and whatever more are likely to far outweigh the value of the original bequest to St Mary's Church made by David Ames, the Testator.

The Church has its bequest, albeit three years late. The Executor, now Alistair personally, will undoubtedly have to pay heavily from his own pocket for his 'assumption' that he was acting in good faith on their late father's behalf. The cost to him will almost certainly be more than the £3,000 legacy to the Church.

An expensive and salutary lesson!

Executors must act according to the specific terms of a Will. That is their responsibility.

It is possible to change requests by Variation. A beneficiary can, in writing and properly witnessed, chose to do so. In this case the beneficiary was never consulted and the Executors acted illegally, whatever their perceived 'higher motives'. The Church acted absolutely within its legal rights. Emotions are one thing – the law is binding.

Chapter 10 covers this subject succinctly. The rules, and limited options, are clearly stated there.

11

And Finally

This book has been written to help guide you through the process of administering the Estate of someone who was probably close to you in some way, following their recent death. Sympathetically and empathetically, we have tried to address the issues that Executors and Administrators face from both emotional and practical aspects.

At the end of this chapter is a theoretical practical example of a typical final account for your guidance. Almost the end of your mission!

The authors have both, to use current parlance, 'been there'. Those who have provided our case histories have added greatly to our awareness of this area of life – and death. Thankfully it does not confront people every day but, for most of us, it is an experience which will probably be faced at some stage.

At the end of each case history you will have read suggestions as to how matters might have been better handled. Some of the issues involved were simpler than others.

We have suggested at certain points throughout the book that there are circumstances when the Executor should consider taking professional advice, even to the extent of handling the whole matter through a solicitor. Such circumstances might include, for example, confrontations through serious family arguments or even contests over the terms of the Will and inheritances, or in valuations of the perceived worth of the Estate.

Fees incurred will be a charge against the estate and thereby reduce the ultimate value for distribution were it to be necessary to employ the services of an appropriate professional.

Executors, as indicated in earlier chapters, could be personally liable for claims of negligence in the handling of the Probate. Where the Executor has decided that a professional adviser has to be employed and paid out of the funds ultimately due to the Estate, should negligence be proved then that professional adviser would be considered as a 'party' to any legal proceedings which might be taken against the Executor.

These circumstances seldom happen, but if you are in a very difficult situation and feel the need to resort to professionals it is important that you make it known to them that you are aware of the realities of the law as concerns you and your paid adviser.

With this caveat we know many people have handled Probate and Administration themselves.

The objective here has been to encourage those facing the task, or anticipating it in the future, to be aware of the processes involved, to look at potential pitfalls and to have the confidence to proceed on their own as appropriate to maximize the proceeds from an Estate, rather than pay out large sums where this might not really have been necessary.

People have shared their experiences, good and bad, with the authors. We shall continue to be interested to hear of new ones. If you have one that you feel might be relevant and helpful to others, please contact the publishers who will pass them on to us for future use.

Example of a final account

Once you have collected all the information that you need regarding assets and liabilities it is a straightforward matter to establish the final worth of the Estate. Using the checklists illustrated at the ends of Chapters 4 and 5, or whatever system you have devised for yourself, you simply add up all the assets and deduct the liabilities to arrive at the value for distribution.

It is good practice to categorize the various elements and the following table is a guide as to how you might present the known facts.

Example of a Final Account

Estate of A. Person – Draft Valuation	Debts	*Assets*
Property		
Detached Bungalow – 36 Hillview – Hemney		*231,000*
Renault Clio Car – P364JLM – 5,000 miles		*10,000*
Insurances		
Endowment Policy (with Profits) – Sun Alliance Policy AD-6784231		*13,500*
Whole Life Insurance – Norwich Union Policy hjB-5640982		*25,000*
Investments		
Building Society – Halifax – Account No. 675463		*5,000*
Shares – various – see attached list		*8,000*
Investment Bonds – AXA Equity & Law – D10098001–140		*21,000*
Valuables – Antiques		
Kneehole desk		*1,000*
Persian Rug 12' x 10' approx		*2,500*
– Jewellery		
Gold Cufflinks – 22 carat		*250*
Rolex, Watch		*2,000*
– Others (collections, paintings, books, stamps, etc)		
5 Oil Paintings by Boydon Bendal		*3,500*
Miscellaneous – includes cash in Current Account – Lloyds		*2,250*
Total gross estate value (approx.)		*325,000*

Estate of A. Person – Draft Valuation	Debts	Assets
Liabilities (Debts)		
Funeral expenses	1,800	
Bills and invoices owing at death	1,550	
Other expenses	150	
Subtotal	3,500	
Probate fees	600	
Income tax outstanding	100	
Total liabilities	4,800	320,200
Less inheritance tax allowance		231,000
Value for IHT consideration		89,200
IHT @ 40%		35,680
Net value for distribution (approx.)		53,520

Appendices

Appendix 1

Working Flowchart for Executors

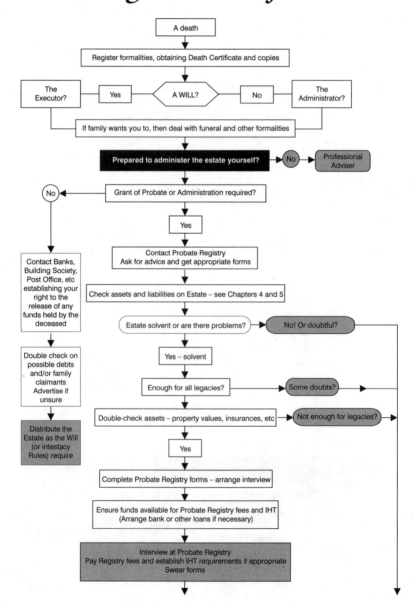

A death

Register formalities, obtaining Death Certificate and copies

The Executor? — Yes — A WILL? — No — The Administrator?

If family wants you to, then deal with funeral and other formalities

Prepared to administer the estate yourself? → No → Professional Adviser

Grant of Probate or Administration required? → No

Yes

Contact Probate Registry
Ask for advice and get appropriate forms

Contact Banks, Building Society, Post Office, etc establishing your right to the release of any funds held by the deceased

Check assets and liabilities on Estate – see Chapters 4 and 5

Estate solvent or are there problems? → No! Or doubtful?

Double check on possible debts and/or family claimants Advertise if unsure

Yes – solvent

Enough for all legacies? → Some doubts?

Distribute the Estate as the Will (or intestacy Rules) require

Double-check assets – property values, insurances, etc → Not enough for legacies?

Yes

Complete Probate Registry forms – arrange interview

Ensure funds available for Probate Registry fees and IHT
(Arrange bank or other loans if necessary)

Interview at Probate Registry
Pay Registry fees and establish IHT requirements if appropriate
Swear forms

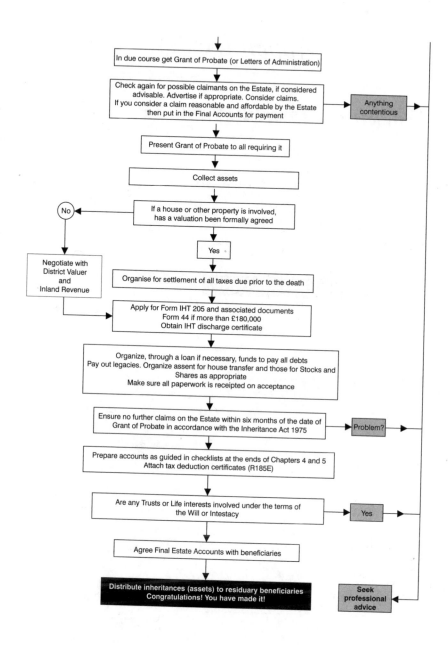

Working Flowchart for Executors (cont)

Appendix 2

When Someone Dies Overseas

As the world shrinks through ever more accessible transport, this happens more often than most people imagine. People die while holidaying or on business abroad. It can be especially distressing.

Obviously more complications are presented than would be the case with a death on home soil, though they need not be too difficult to cope with. However, if it is wished to bring the body home the process can be fraught with difficulties and is always expensive.

Who informs the appropriate authorities?

The death will have to be registered in accordance with the laws of the country where the death has occurred.

Should a next of kin have been accompanying the deceased, on holiday for example, the death should be registered with the British Embassy, High Commission or Consul in that country. If the death happened on a business trip it is to be hoped that the employer would handle all appropriate arrangements. The Ministry of Defence will handle deaths of active service personnel abroad, besides bearing some of the cost.

A death at sea on a British registered vessel – and this includes small pleasure craft – is considered as having occurred 'at home'. On a foreign registered vessel it is considered as 'abroad'. In either instance it must be recorded by the person in charge of the vessel and reported on arrival at the port where the deceased's body is to be landed. If the landing is at a British port it must be reported to the local coroner. If overseas, local laws will apply and this is where it is important also to ensure that the British government representative there is informed. Similarly, following a death in an aircraft, the captain must inform local police on the next landing and the registration authority in the country to which the aircraft belongs.

Whatever the circumstances of the death, and in whichever country, it is important that the local British Consul is informed for registration purposes. Only in this way can a certified copy of the death certificate be ultimately obtained from the General Register Office in the UK, which could be an important document for the Executor to have available.

Making the funeral arrangements

It is possible to arrange for a funeral to take place in the country where the death occurred, since repatriation of the deceased to the UK can be an extremely costly business which the bereaved might simply be unable to afford.

If the deceased was covered by travel insurance, for instance as part of a package holiday arrangement, relatives are usually able to recover the costs, although repatriation is an extremely complex and often long-winded process, and anyone placed in this situation is strongly advised to arrange for a UK firm of funeral directors to make all the necessary arrangements. Many are well-versed in the practicalities of this and the maze of paperwork required, which of course varies from country to country.

Appendix 3

Probate Registries and Capital Taxes Office

Controlling Probate Registry
Open to the public 9.30 am – 4.00 pm
Mondays to Fridays

Local offices
Consult controlling
office for addresses
and opening times
(*by appointment only*)

Bangor	1st Floor Council Offices Ffordd Gwynedd LL57 1YS 01248 362410	Rhyl Wrexham
Birmingham	The Priory Courts 33 Bull Street Birmingham B4 6DU 0121 681 3400	Coventry Kidderminster Lichfield Northampton Wolverhampton
Bodmin	Market Street Bodmin PL31 2JW 01208 72279	Plymouth Truro
Brighton	William Street Brighton BN2 2LG 01273 684071	Chichester Crawley Hastings
Bristol	The Crescent Centre Temple Back Bristol BS1 6EP 0117 927 3915/926 4619	Bath Weston-Super-Mare

Cardiff	Probate Registry of Wales PO Box 474 2 Park Street Cardiff CF1 1TB 01222 376479	Bridgend Newport Pontypridd
Carlisle	Courts of Justice Earl Street Carlisle CA1 1DJ 01228 521751	
Carmarthen	14 King Street Carmarthen Dyfed SA31 1BL 01267 236238	Aberystwyth Haverfordwest Swansea
Chester	5th Floor Hamilton House Hamilton Place Chester CH1 2DA 01244 345082	
Exeter	Finance House Barnfield Road Exeter Devon EX1 1QR 01392 274515	Barnstaple Newton Abbot/Torquay Plymouth Taunton Yeovil
Gloucester	2nd Floor Combined Court Building Kimbrose Way Gloucester GL1 2DG 01452 522585	Cheltenham Hereford Worcester
Ipswich	Level 3 Haven House 17 Lower Brook Street Ipswich IP4 1DN 01473 253724/259261	Chelmsford Colchester
Lancaster	Mitre House Church Street Lancaster LA1 1HE 01524 36625	Barrow-in-Furness Blackpool Preston

Leeds	3rd Floor Coronet House Queen Street Leeds LS1 2BA 0113 243 1505	Bradford Huddersfield Wakefield
Leicester	5th Floor Leicester House Lee Circle Leicester LE1 3RE 0116 253 8558	Bedford
Lincoln	Mill House Brayford Side North Lincoln LN1 1YW 01522 523648	Grimsby
Liverpool	The Queen Elizabeth II Law Courts Derby Square Liverpool L2 1XA 0151 236 8264	Southport St Helens Wallasey
London	Principal Registry of the Family Division Ground Floor First Avenue House 42–49 High Holborn London WC1V 6NP 0171 936 6983	Croydon Edmonton Harlow Kingston Luton Southend-on-Sea Woolwich

Personal enquiries Ground Floor, Search Room
10.00 am – 4.30 pm Monday to Friday

Maidstone	The Law Courts Barker Road Maidstone ME16 8EW 01622 202048/7	Canterbury Chatham Tunbridge Wells
Manchester	9th Floor Astley House 23 Quay Street Manchester M3 4AT 0161 834 4319	Bolton Nelson Oldham Warrington Wigan

Middlesbrough Centre	(see also Russell Street Middlesbrough TS1 2AE 01642 340001	Combined Court Newcastle-upon-Tyne)
Newcastle-upon-Tyne	2nd Floor Plummer House Croft Street Newcastle-upon-Tyne NE1 6NP 0191 261 8383	
Norwich	Combined Court Building The Law Courts Bishopsgate Norwich NR3 1UR 01603 761776 Ext. 2126	Lowestoft
Nottingham	Butt Dyke House 33 Park Row Nottingham NG1 6GR 0115 941 4288	Derby Mansfield
Oxford	10A New Road Oxford OX1 1LY 01865 241163/247432	Aylesbury High Wycombe Reading Slough Swindon
Peterborough	Crown Buildings Rivergate Peterborough PE1 1EJ 01733 562802	Cambridge King's Lynn
Sheffield	PO Box 832 The Law Courts 50 West Bar Sheffield S3 8YR 0114 281 2596	Chesterfield Doncaster

Stoke-on-Trent	Combined Court Centre Bethesda Street Hanley Stoke-on-Trent ST1 3BP 01782 854065	Crewe Shrewsbury Stafford
Winchester	4th Floor Cromwell House Andover Road Winchester SO23 7EW 01962 853046/863771	Basingstoke Bournemouth Dorchester Guildford Newport IOW Portsmouth Salisbury Southampton
York	Duncombe Place York YO1 2EA 01904 624210/671564	Hull Scarborough

Capital Taxes Office

PO Box 38
Ferrers House
Nottingham NG2 1BB
0115 974 2400

Appendix 4

Cash Book Diary

	EXPENSES	£
Date	**Details**	
28/9 Aug	Phone calls – including relation Australia	16.50
29/30 Aug	Mileage – Registrar, Undertakers etc – @ £x per mile	20.00
Various	Postage	10.00
Various	Photocopies – Death Cert. + other	6.00
5 Sept	Undertakers	1,328.75
14 Sept	Funeral 'Tea' – general catering cost	158.65
14 Sept	Heating Oil Bill	70.00
20 Sept	Clear Bank Overdraft – No. 2 A/c	21.28
20 Sept	Settle 2 small local traders bills	30.40
31 Oct	Electricity Bill	138.60
2 Dec	Final Electricity Bill	32.40
4 Dec	Donation to Animal Sanctuary for care	
	of family pet	50.00
4 Dec	Distribute minor legacies per requests	
	written in Will (see sep sheet)	4,750
5 Dec	Further phone calls and postage	23.60
5 Dec	Additional mileage @ £x per mile	30.00
	TOTAL carried forward	

	RECEIPTS	
Date	Details	£
31 Aug	Cash found in home	450
15 Sept	Redeem Premium Bonds	250
26 Sept	Sale of 1992 Ford Fiesta	1150
30 Sept	Life Policy St Life	7843
8 Oct	Shares sold (see sep sheet)	3193
20 Oct	Close Midland Bank – Current	675
30 Oct	Refund Council Tax	158
2 Dec	Net sale of bungalow after fees to Solicitors and Estate Agents	75,738
	TOTAL carried forward	

Notes: to do/Check

6 Sept	Chase Bank Manager
15 Sept	Meeting Local Council Office
Remember	Check share price movements daily and discuss weekly with daughters re decision on time sell at best for their max.

NB: this example is deliberately unfinished as its purpose is merely to offer guidance on the sort of 'elements' to look for. Every Executor will find their own way of accounting, though we do recommend that you adopt a disciplined approach. Trying to 'pick up the pieces' towards the end is far more time-consuming and can cause problems. The principle of the Cash Book Diary is that expenses are shown as they were incurred and are therefore more readily understandable.

Appendix 5

Simple Example of a Written Will

This book has explained the importance of people making their Will, and some of the hazards they can leave behind for others if they do not. A specific example of a Will follows on the next three pages. It is most important to recognise that no two Wills should necessarily be alike. Even husbands and wives drafting Wills at the same time might want differing clauses, for whatever reason.

This is not to be viewed as a 'template' where names and a few other words can be altered. The making of a Will, even for those thinking of themselves as having only the most modest assets to leave, needs thought and the modest cost of professional advice taken when making the Will can be a fine legacy in itself. Written with professional consultation, and with considerations for the benefit of future generations, family feuds might be avoided and, importantly, more money retained through tax-efficient planning.

The sample shown is based on Parker's Modern Wills Precendents, 3rd Edition, © Eric Taylor 1997, (Butterworths), and we are grateful for permission to reproduce it here.

LAST WILL AND TESTAMENT

THIS WILL dated November One thousand nine hundred and ninety seven is made by me FREDERICK GEORGE HANDEL of 26 Railway Cuttings, East Cheam, Surrey KT99 4DD.

1   I revoke all earlier Wills and Codicils.

2.1   I appoint my wife SUSANNAH CAROLINE HANDEL and my Friend JOHN WASHINGTON to be the Executors of this my Will.

2.2   If an Executor is unable or unwilling to act then I appoint my Friend OLIVER CROMWELL to act and I appoint as my Trustees those of my Executors who obtain probate of this my Will.

2.3   In this Will 'my Trustees' means those of my Executors who obtain probate and the Trustees for the time being of any trust arising under this Will.

2.4   Any of my Trustees (other than my spouse) being a professional person may charge fees for work done and time expended by him or his firm (whether or not the work is of a professional nature) on the same basis as if he we were not one of my Trustees but employed to carry out the work on their behalf.

3   If my wife SUSANNAH CAROLINE HANDEL survives me by 30 days I give the whole of my Estate to her but if this gift fails the following provisions of my Will shall apply.

4   Should I survive my Wife SUSANNAH CAROLINE HANDEL then I appoint my cousin WENDY PAN to be the guardian of any of my children who are under the age of 18 at the date of my death.

5   My Trustees shall hold my Estate on trust for sale on the following terms:

5.1   To pay debts and executorship fees;

5.2   To pay Inheritance Tax in respect of property passing under this Will;

5.3   To hold the residue ('the Trust Fund') on the following discretionary trust:

5.3.1   To apply the capital of the Trust Fund for the benefit of any such of my children as my Trustees think fit;

5.3.2 To apply the income of the Trust Fund for the benefit of such of my children as my Trustees think fit or (for not more than 21 years from my death) to accumulate all or any part of it;

5.3.3 When all my children have attained 25 or died under that age to end the Trust by distributing the Trust Fund among such of my children as my Trustees think fit;

5.3.4 If any of my children dies before me or while this Trust is in existence his children shall be included among those in whose favour my Trustees may exercise their discretion;

5.3.5 My Trustees may exercise their discretionary powers when and how they think fit and need not make payments to or for the benefit of all those in whose favour they can exercise their discretion nor ensure equality among those who are benefited.

5.4 My Trustees shall have the following powers:

5.4.1 To retain or sell any of the assets constituting the Trust Fund;

5.4.2 To invest as if they were beneficially entitled and this power includes the right to invest:

    (a) in unsecured interest-free loans to any discretionary beneficiary;

    (b) in non-income producing assets including policies of life assurance (with power to pay premiums out of income or capital);

5.4.3 To use the income or capital of the Trust Fund for or towards the cost of maintaining or improving any property forming part of the Trust Fund;

5.4.4 To insure any asset of the Trust Fund on such terms as they think fit and:

    (a) to pay premiums out of income or capital;

    (b) to use any insurance money received to restore the asset or to apply it as if it were the proceeds of its sale;

5.4.5 To borrow money on such terms as they think fit and to use it for any purpose for which the capital of the Trust Fund may be used;

5.4.6 To do anything incidental to the powers which my Trustees have whether given by statute or under this Will;

5.4.7 To hold investments in the name of such person or such body as they think fit.

6 I wish my body to be buried in the Mariners Cemetery at WHITBY, North Yorkshire.

Signed

....

Signed by the Testator in the presence of us at the same time who at his request and in his presence and in the presence of each other have subscribed our names as witnesses.

....

Signature   Signature

Name   Name

Address   Address

Occupation   Occupation

Date   Date

Page 3 of 3

Glossary of Common Legal Terms

Many in the legal profession, along with some government departments, are making significant progress in pursuing a campaign for the use of 'plain English' in official documentation. Despite the efforts of those dedicated to the cause, you are still likely to come across words, definitions and phrases in use which are absurd, unnecessarily lengthy and often quite simply 'gobbledegook' to the layman.

Where you come across words starting with a capital letter (eg Executors, Trustees) these are words which are defined within the Will and carry that meaning throughout the document.

It is hoped that this appendix will help to explain some of the more frequently used terms that you are likely to encounter.

Absolute. Describing something without condition.

Ademption. The cancellation or reduction of a gift specified in a Will because it is no longer wholly owned by the Testator at the time of death, the Testator has already disposed of all or part of it before death or there is nothing fitting its description in the Will. For example, should a Testator leave a house that was sold during his or her lifetime, or if after making a Will leaving it to a child the Testator gives the child property constituting a portion of the property, the legacy is in each case 'adeemed'. The gift of the house is cancelled and the child's legacy is reduced by the amount of the portion.

Administrator. Someone who is appointed to undertake the duties of organizing the affairs of the deceased, settling any debts and distributing any assets where the deceased has died without making a Will.

Asset. Anything owned such as property, car, furniture, pictures, jewellery, stocks and shares and other possessions including bank accounts and the value accruing from any insurance policies.

Assent. A document by which Executors/Personal Representatives transfer property, whether freehold or leasehold, to a beneficiary. No transfer of title is complete until this has been effected.

Beneficiary. A person/persons or an organization such as a named charity inheriting either through a Will or Intestacy; also those named to receive money, property or possessions under a trust.

Benefits Agency. Part of the Department of Social Security. Their Recovery from Estates Department monitors Grants of Probate. Should they consider that assets were hidden at the time that a claim was made, they demand refunds from the Estate of claims paid out.

Bequests. A gift, usually specified, other than land or property.

Bond of caution (only in Scottish law). Money set aside to compensate the Estate for loss caused by an Executor's error or omission.

Chargeable Gift. Anything left or given under the terms of a Will or during a person's lifetime which is liable for tax.

Children. The definition of children in a Will covers both the legitimate and illegitimate, and also those legally adopted by the parent or parents. All such children have the same rights should their parents die Intestate. This does not apply to stepchildren, though they can be specified in a Will.

Changes in our laws happen quite rapidly and some that you might have assumed applied are sometimes overruled by High Court judgments, or the European Court of Human Rights.

You often read about seemingly bizarre cases in newspapers or see them reported on television. Changes happen in our lifetimes, sometimes quite rapidly.

A very topical aspect here is worthy of consideration. Genetic engineering and fertilization treatment, in all manifestations currently known, and anticipating the probably inevitable future developments, create a potential legal minefield when it comes to the writing of a Will and the ultimate right to inheritances. The present position is covered by the Human Fertilization and Embryology Act 1990 and an Executor, or Administrator if there is no Will, aware of such a background should consult a solicitor who is specialized in this complex area of the law. With medical science developments increasing rapidly there may well be even more complex problems that the lawyers and Executors will be facing.

Codicil. A clause or clauses which alter a Will, sometimes written on the Will itself, or appended. These should be avoided, as a full rewrite, making a new 'Final Will', is very simple to do, and inexpensive. It should also ensure that there is less opportunity for misunderstanding or challenge.

Confirmation. A Grant of Probate in Scottish law.

Court. Where a court is referred to in this book it will usually be the County Court. Generally it is that court that handles matters relating to what are considered relatively small amounts, under £50,000. For substantial amounts the High Court may have to be involved.

Deceased. The person who has died.

Descendants. Family from your direct blood line; children, grandchildren; can in certain circumstances include nephews and nieces, etc.

Devise (and bequeath). To give a gift of property, a building or land, under a Will. (See *Bequest.*)

Distribution. The final handing over of a part, or all, of an Estate to the beneficiaries named in a Will following the granting of Probate, or Letters of Administration in the instance of Intestacy.

Docket. In Scottish law, a formal note.

Engrossment. The final copy of a legal document ready for signature.

Estate. The property of the deceased.

Excepted Estate (see Chapter 6). Where the value of the Estate is such that there is no requirement to submit the Inland Revenue Account form.

Executor. A person appointed in the Will by the Testator to deal with their Estate after their death.

Gifts. *1. Absolute Gift*, eg 'I leave my hi-fi and recorded music collection to my daughter Elizabeth'. *2. Conditional Gift*, eg 'I leave my golf clubs and trophy collection to my son Peter on the condition that he remains an active and paid up member of the ABC Golf Club to the date of my death'.

Indenture. A deed, generally one creating or transferring an estate in land (eg a conveyance or lease).

Heritable Property. The Scottish law definition for land or buildings.

Infant or Minor. The legal term for a person under the age of 18. In current law they cannot acquire assets from an Estate until this age unless the Will specifies an earlier age. It is common practice for assets to be bequeathed under the terms of a trust until the 'age of majority' is reached. Often a Testator might specify that the Estate, or part of it, be held in trust until the beneficiary, or beneficiaries, are much older than 18.

IHT. Inheritance tax.

Interest. The right to all or part of the deceased's assets.

Intestate. Dying, having left no valid Will.

Issue. Another word used for direct, blood line descendants.

Legacy. A gift, other than a house or land, left to someone in a Will; a bequest.

Legal Rights. In Scottish law the surviving spouse, and/or children, are entitled to any benefits from the net Estate regardless of the terms of the Will or intestacy rules. If the deceased's children have predeceased them, grandchildren, or even other relatives, can be beneficiaries. English law is increasingly moving in this direction and there are now limited rights, at least for the bereaved spouse. (See Chapter 8.)

Life Interest. A Testator can state in their Will that a house, land, money or any other possession can be used and enjoyed by a named individual, or others specified, for their lifetime. Unless the item is to pass onto another person after the life tenant has died, on the death of someone so named the value of the asset reverts to the Testator's estate and would be liable for IHT, if appropriate. Unless specific provision is made in the Will the capital cannot be touched.

Life Tenant. Someone named to enjoy the benefits as outlined above. This could include the right to live in a house, collect or keep rents from lettings or benefit from dividends or interest derived from investments during their lifetime. However, the capital asset remains part of the deceased's Estate. (See also **Tenant.**)

Moveable Property. Quite simply a term for any of the deceased's former possessions other than buildings or land.

Next of Kin. The closest living blood relative.

Pecuniary Legacy. A gift of money in a Will to a named person or organization.

Personal Representative. Someone managing the financial affairs of a person who has died; an Executor if so named in a Will; someone appointed by the Probate Registry, following appropriate application, to deal with an Estate in a Grant of Representation; if not appointed by being named in a Will then referred to as an Administrator.

Prior Rights. Under Scottish law this covers one of the sets of rights regarding a deceased's property. In particular they determine what the surviving spouse receives in the case of Intestacy.

Probate. The formal document issued by the Probate Registry which confirms the validity of the Will and authorizes the Executor(s) to act on the deceased's behalf.

Residue. After all taxes, debts, expenses, legacies and bequests have been paid out, what remains in the Estate is referred to as the residue.

Small Estate. In England and Wales this is, at current levels, considered to have a gross value of less than £5000. It is possible to distribute the Estate without the formality of applying for a Grant of Probate. In Scotland a 'Small Estate' is currently considered to have a gross value of less than £17,000.

Specific Gifts. The gift of a specific asset – in essence as simple as that. The Administration of Estates Act 1925 provides an extensive list by way of definition, much of which would rather seem irrelevant in the latter part of the 1990s. In essence it covers all the normally expected household effects used today, including books, pictures, furniture, china, glass, musical instruments, photographic equipment, home computers, jewellery and other items of personal use or ornament, wines, liquors and other consumables. Also included are domestic animals.

The Act excluded items used for business purposes such as cars and other equipment or accessories, money or securities for money. Nowadays these are commonly included in the definition.

All embracing phrases, such as 'I leave the contents of my house to...', written into a Will could cause problems if it had been intended to gift one or more particular items to beneficiaries, or if a large sum of cash was kept in the home that was not intended for the beneficiary of the 'physical' contents (personal chattels).

Survivor. In a partnership, married or unmarried, the person still alive at the time of the Testator's death. Usually they will be a beneficiary under the terms of a Will. However, Wills can and are sometimes written in such a way that the surviving spouse, or partner, is *not* to be a beneficiary of the Testator's Estate. The reasons for this should have been carefully discussed, planned and reasoned at the time of the Will being written and are designed to protect assets for future generations, or identified closer family. Often they are designed in the interests of perceived 'fairness' where a 'new family' is created following remarriage after death or divorce and attempt to avoid unpleasant squabbles in the future. Tax considerations might be important and there is nothing sinister in being tax-efficient.

Tenant. In dealing with property disposals the Executor, or Personal Representative, could be faced with three options:

1. *Joint tenants* (legally described as Tenants in Equity *or* Tenants in fee simple *or* Beneficial Joint Tenants). To the layman this means that when two people own a property jointly then on the death of one of them the property is already owned by the survivor.

2. *Tenants in Common.* Where two, or more, people own specified shares in the value of a property. In the case of married couples this was generally done on a 50/50 basis. Today, however, there are many examples of ownership in different proportions perhaps as a result of second marriages or unmarried partners providing unequal shares in the equity and wishing to preserve that percentage to be left to others through their Will. Unlike with a Joint Tenancy, each co-owner's share does not pass automatically to the other owners on his or her death.

   This share might be gifted in the Will to Trustees for the benefit of any offspring or named relative with the stipulation that the share, of whatever percentage, must not be sold or otherwise disposed of during the lifetime of a survivor without full consent. Should a survivor(s) wish, and formally agree, then the property may be sold and the proceeds used to purchase another property. The share in the new property is considered as held in Trust.

   There can be certain advantages to owning a property in this way, even though it may seem complex. The possibilities of IHT liabilities can be reduced, or avoided, by protecting the percentage share of the value of a property destined, ultimately, for the benefit of children. This legal device is often used in the event of a survivor remarrying. It can also protect the proportional interest of ultimate beneficiaries of an Estate in the event of a survivor being taken into care.

3. *Life Tenancy*. Where a named person, or persons, is granted the right to live in the property either for their lifetime or a specified number of years. This 'tenancy' will usually state that they should be responsible for the maintenance of the property to a proper standard, including insuring it, unless other financial provision is made available under the terms of the Will.

On the Tenant's death, or at the end of the specified period, the property will pass in accordance with the terms of the Testator's Will.

Testamentary Expenses. Reasonable costs incurred in the administration of the Estate such as postage, telephone usage, petrol, etc. No professional fees can be claimed against the Estate unless provision is made in the Will for them.

Testator. A person who has made a lawful Will, has had their signature properly witnessed, and then has died.

Trusts. Under a Will, where the Testator leaves assets to Trustees (see below) to hold for the benefit of one or more persons (the Beneficiaries). The Trustees have legal ownership of the assets but can only deal with them in accordance with strict trust law and the powers given to them under the Will and must always have regard to the needs of the Beneficiaries. If they do not, a Beneficiary can enforce the Trust by legal action. A Trust will be established for infants/minors (see above) and often for tax-saving purposes.

Trustees. Where two or more people are given the legal responsibility for administering an Estate, in accordance with the stated wishes of the deceased in a Will, for the maximum benefit of the beneficiaries. Usually the Trustees of a deceased's estate are the same as the Executors. Trustees have ('nominal' ownership of all or part of the deceased's Estate until such time, as stated in the Will, that the Estate is handed over.

Index

Please use in conjunction with the Glossary of Common Legal Terms, pages 177–84

Index

Index of Advertisers